Mir

MW00980611

Manifesting Marvels, Miracles and Mysteries

Soulscape

Words are, in my not-so-humble opinion,
our most inexhaustible source of magic.
Capable of both inflicting injury
and remedying it.

J. K. Rowling

Linda Varsell Smith

Thanks to

Maureen Frank: The Mandala Lady
for formatting the manuscript for printing
and designing the covers and interior art.

My poetry friends, critique groups.
intuitive consultants and family.

ISBN: 978-0-9888554-8-9

Rainbow Communications
471 NW Hemlock Ave.
Corvallis, OR 97330

varsell4@comcast.net

Linda Varsell Smith is a poet, novelist, teacher who seeks the mirabilia of the multiverse. She lives in Corvallis, Oregon with her husband Court in a mini-museum. She is a retired English teacher of creative writing, children's literature, literary publication which created Linn-Benton Community College's The Eloquent Umbrella creative arts magazine. She was an editor at Calyx Books for over 30 years, former president of the Oregon Poetry Association and current president of PEN Women Portland. She plays competitive and cooperative Scrabble, is a member of Poetic License, Marys Peak Poets, teaches workshops, sponsors youth writing events and is part of the Writing the Wrongs Huddle composed of poets and children's book writers.

Table of Contents

That that is to be so soon, and under circumstances as joyful,
are among the mirabilia of this changing world. George Eliot

Cosmic Miracles

Gifts of Gaia

Ancient Mysteries

Quotidian Discoveries

Exploring Intentions and Marvels

Creative Magic

Wondrous Spirituality

Connecting Hope for a Mirabilous Future

The most beautiful thing we can experience is the mysterious. It is the sources of all true art and science.

Albert Einstein

Cosmic Miracles

Alpha Centauri

There was a star
riding clouds one night,
and I said to the star
"consume me."
Virginia Woolf

Stellar Mysteries

Be humble for you are made of earth. Be noble for you are made of stars.
Serbian Proverb

Earth and inhabitants are made of star stuff.
Humble or noble we are all from same source--
a Creator of matter, darkness and light.
All a mystery to us, of course.

We each have our opinion
how things came to be,
how to use our sentience
and live creatively.

In our every day lives
for most ordinary people
we might not consider our acts
either humble or noble.

Making choices and judgments
or being cosmically free
to let go to the universe
requires intentionality.

We are in a low-vibe destination
with a fragile body encasing a heart-mind.
Our interpretations elicit feelings
not always luminous, I find.

The concept of All is splendiferous,
our stellar origins could enlight
a sense of knowing or keep us guessing.
I've accepted I haven't guessed right.

The Omni-Sparkler

I do believe we're all connected.
I do believe in positive energy.
I do believe in the power of prayer.
I do believe in putting good out into the world.
And I believe in taking care of each other.
Harvey Firestein

When the Omni-Sparkler sparked existence
of energy and matter throughout the multiverse,
how did the Omni-Sparkler originate?
How did the Omni-Sparkler create
all the codes, patterns, quantum quarks
causing collisions, conglomerations,
cosmic experiments with various goals,
configurations, degrees of consciousness?

The vast scale, complexity is beyond our comprehension.
We lack the ability and equipment to figure it all out.
Are people just a minuscule ort
in some evolving spiritual, scientific experiment?
Our coded, circuit boards, DNA
wired before birth by some entity?
How about inserting Earth-game rules?
How much wiggle room do we have—
just a cog in a wheel?
Do we know if we pass the test? Win the game?
Judged by some cosmic hierarchy?

How much we connect, exude positive energy,
activate prayerful sequences,
put out good in the world and care for others
might be only one track or one game plan.
For others, a negative goal line competes?
I'll try to select the light line.
I'm in the dark about so much already.
I'll catch and spark as much light as I can.

Inventing the Multiverse

What is the origin of the multiverse?
Was it created to be so perverse? Diverse?

Untestably philosophical
or speculatively theological?

Some determined physicists insist
their "baby universe" could exist.

Can a physicist hacker create
a big bang? Causes some debate.

Can we play God and create a new universe?
Wonder if I'd be better or worse?

Does it require higher intelligence than us
to pattern such a cosmic omnibus?

Our laws of physics would apply?
Or maybe new ones get a try?

Quantum mechanics of Big Bang holds indications
for life after death and resurrection speculations?

Some ponder if God is happy,
"consciousness field" possibility.

Just what can we expect
if inflation theory is correct?

Will baby universes birth more?
How can we observe and explore?

Are our laws of physics fundamental
or elsewhere considered experimental?

Just have to trust on faith without evidence?
Does exotic new physics promise credence?

Is this just post-truth nonsense?
What do we know of significance?

Still scientists spend a lot of time
trying to duplicate the sublime.

Cosmic Coup

Whether we are a simulation game,
hologram or some cosmic experiment
in the control of some dominating force,
it is time for a cosmic coup.

Maybe we need a change in controllers,
maybe a tweak in the rules of the experiment?
Maybe a new planetary, galactic
or multiversal scenario?

It seems after all this time since creation
some energy should have found out what works
and some consciousness could have developed
a less violent, more just game or tests.

What is wrong with knowing what's going on?
Why are we in the dark as well as dark matter
and dark energy? What else is kept from us?
Why this cosmic cycle of unknowing and guessing?

Are we really on a love trip on Earth?
It does not look like we are passing the test
despite all our pleas to deities and E.T.'s.
We could face extinction with or without input.

There are billions of us with lethal technology,
inequities in resource distribution, violent tendencies.
Overwhelming challenges face sentient beings.
I am exhausted trying to figure it all out.

Even if I do, others would also have to
for a shift in attitude and aptitude.
Despite New Age gurus trying to raise our frequencies,
some religions are crying apocalypse.

Are we a cosmic whack or scientific accident
from annihilation? What will the gamers
and controllers do? Start again with different criteria
of how existence can be happier, safer? Or not?

The Cosmic Check List

How many lives does the multiverse allot?
How does one get a preferable slot?
Did I know the answer and I forgot?

How does one get on the exist list?
Does anyone give an assist?
Is it futile to resist?

Are all options explorable?
Are any choices ignorable?
Can choose adorable or deplorable?

Are souls eternally on the go?
Part of the sentience energy flow?
Is there any way one gets to know?

Some beings have closer cosmic connections?
Some sense better selections?
Some will get clearer directions?

Earthbound guidelines: pro or anti guru?
For a price they tell you what to do?
What do the poor people do?

Do different dimensions have different rules?
Diverse habitats and altered genetic pools?
Free will or controlled- what are the tools?

If we are soul-slivers of the divine
and inside us all is a direct line,
how does one mine this "mine"?

The multiverse is so complex,
way beyond google-plex,
who keeps track of all the specs?

Can anyone answer the mysterious questions?
Consciousness reveals some suggestions?
Cosmic hot line holds multiple congestions?

Questioning Dark Matter

What's
Dark Matter?
Invisible Puppet Master?

Unseen
Cosmic Ghosts?
Pure energy particles?

Are
they WIMPS?
Family of particles?

Does
Dark Matter
cause Earth's extinctions?

Every
30 million
years, a repeat?

We
are possibly
from Dark Matter?

Puppet
Master's patterns
thread sticky webs?

Filaments
of galaxies
form this web?

Pulls
normal matter
into this structure?

Vera
Rubin sees
galactic spinning wheel?

How'll
we measure?
Can't see, feel?

Does
not interact
with light? Gravity?

Think
Dark Matter
interacts with gravity?

Quantum
world fluctuates
into dense points?

Big
Bang burst
86% Dark Matter?

Pure
energy– subatomic
from Big Bang?

Gases
collapse into
stars and mass?

Colliding
energy powers
stars, dark stars?

It
powers Massive
Super Black Holes?

Dark
matter annihilates
when matter collides?

Billions
of stars–
Dark Matter halo?

Dark
Matter disk?
Sun propels comets?

Clusters
when collide
pass through? Smoosh?

Waves
of dark
light–sci fi?

Invisible
world beside
ours? Dark Matter?

Galactic
x-rays indicate
Dark Matter proof?

More
unknown than
known? Many theories?

Dominant
creative force
in universe...us?

Puppet
Master, what
pulls your strings?

Moon

Made from smash with Theia?
Mashed from space debris in area?
Managed to spin into Moon, transformed?
Millions of years as Earth formed?
Many scientists speculate Moon's retrieval.
Muddle about Moon's speculated arrival.
Mutter about our Earth's survival.

Musk's Moon Trip

SpaceX founder Elon Musk
plans to fly two private citizens
around the moon for a week in 2018.

These select two would fly
deeper into space than any human before.
Real Star Trek stuff.

This lunar journey would not land.
No tourists since Neil Armstrong's trip
have touched the moon's surface.

Musk will not reveal the two passengers
on this flight. Must be rich to afford it.
He just said they're not stars—celebrities.

His space ventures ended
governments' monopoly in space.
SpaceX has not flown people before.

Musk ultimately wants to colonize Mars.
He's blown up two rockets in two years.
This mission is on a Falcon Heavy rocket.

Musk has worked with NASA to fly cargo
and eventually fly international crews
to the International Space Station.

If NASA wants to partner with the lunar mission
that would take priority over tourists.
He wants to advance space exploration.

Telescopes and satellites get to explore space.
Will we send two scientists? Poets? CEOs?
What will who we send say about us?

Including Pluto

Some
say
Pluto's
planet again,
not dwarf, but
planet. Any size? Other
spheres could be included?
What balls now excluded? Pluto
returns with moons, other round bodies?
Inclusivity goes universal?

Asgardia

Asgardia: a new space station dedicated to expanding peaceful exploration of space for the benefit of humanity lead by Igor Ashbeyli, chairman of UNESCO's Science of Space Committee and founder of the Aerospace International Research Center in Vienna

You can become a citizen of Asgardia
with an "independent platform free from constraint
of land-based country's laws." Aiming
to launch a satellite in October 2017
on the 60th anniversary of launching Sputnik.

Another goal is to create a protective shield
from threats to life on Earth, such as:
space debris, coronal mass ejections
and asteroids. A big challenge for a satellite!
Worthy motives—elusive execution?

Asgardia proponents want people
to sign up to become citizens.
When applications are over 100,000
the organization plans to apply to the UN
for the status of a state? A space colony?

Asgardia's name has roots in Asgard mythology.
In Norse myth Asgard is one of nine worlds
ruled by Odin. Warriors feast and fight in Valhalla.
Asgard is set in the sky with a rainbow bridge
Bifrost connecting it to Earth. Not a peaceful bunch.

Asgard in the Marvel universe is a world existing
in another dimension about the size of USA.
God Thor created Asgard on Earth. Iron Man
suggested Asgard become a separate nation
like a foreign embassy. Asgardia like fiction?

We do have an International Space Station collaborating
space exploration with governments and private enterprise.
But does it have the magical powers Asgardia hopes to have?
Will Asgardia be myth? Scientific superheroes?
The details for Asgardia remain mystical.

If Asgardia is free from Earthly regulation,
how will they work together? What is to prevent
other satellites with less laudable motives
from launching their own agendas. Not compatible?
Who is liable if something goes wrong on Asgardia?
Asgardia could be a sky-borne state
orbiting above earthly, grounded nations,
free to conduct space research supposedly
to protect its earthbound neighbors.
What if there is a takeover? Attacks Earth?

I'd like to be an optimist, a citizen
of a lofty, laudable state, but
there is a lot of space junk, space debris
needing cleanup. Can Asgardia fulfill
its intentions? Will we build a Bifrost?

Alphabetical Aliens

Aliens believe contact–
destiny eventually,
for galaxies' habitats,
illuminate, just keep
nurturing multidimensional
oversouls, participating quantumly,
resonating sentience,
transforming understanding,
vexing xenophobia–
yonder zenith.

Aliens

Advocate for E.T.s in our areA?
Located here? I await arrivaL.
Individually some believe we're starseeded alumnI
Eventually bubble may burst with our branE?
Never doubt cosmos' plan–eveN
Sever old beliefs for multi-dimensionS?

Discovering Extrasolar Planets

"...when we look at the nearest stars, all of them appear to have planets orbiting them...These new planets also help us better understand the formation of planetary systems to provide interesting targets for future efforts to image the planets directly." Dr. Mikko Tuomi

We can only see a smidgen of stars.
Astronomers looked for over 20 years.
They are looking way beyond Mars;
found over 114 potential new worlds, it appears.
　　　As our telescopes explore,
　　　we will find so many more.

Astronomers looked for over 20 years.
16,000 observations of 1,600 stars to date.
With Keck-1 telescope in Hawaii these star-seers
found several discoveries to celebrate.
　　　Observations part of Lick-Carnegie Exoplanet Survey,
　　　which will document discoveries for display.

They are looking way beyond Mars,
starting at University of California in 1996
with astronomers' stellar seminars,
when Carnegie Institute of Science joined mix.
　　　Patiently viewing red to blue starlight shifts;
　　　they recorded how light sifts.

Found over 114 potential new worlds it appears.
60 new planets orbiting near to Earth's solar system.
54 planets found by University of Herefordshire peers.
Gliese 411b is a hot, super-Earth rocky item.
　　　Scientists look for places our life forms can live,
　　　like putting stardust through a sieve.

As our telescopes explore,
they find rogue or orphan planets tossed
out of some orbit - afloat without an oar.
These planets were star-crossed.
　　　Many planetary varieties we could find--
　　　hopefully some of a benign kind.

We will find so many more
as our technology advances.
We're part of the cosmic dance –a terpsichore,
giving Earth beings more spec-star-ular chances.
　　　Wherever we look up there is the hope
　　　we'll find a place where Earthlings can cope.

Seven Wonders of Trappist-1

With this amazing system, we know there must be many more potentially life-bearing worlds out there just waiting to be found. Sara Seager

Telescopes on the ground and in the sky
found perhaps habitable, Earth-size planets
orbiting a dim, dwarf star 40 light years away.

This Jupiter-sized sun is labeled Trappist-1a.
The seven planets named b-h.
Why not Snow White and seven dwarfs?

Scientists are studying the first four planets.
Inner three considered possibly habitable.
The outer two are probably icy, snowball-like worlds.

They orbit their sun between 1½ to 20 days.
If you saw another of the planets, maybe
about as big as twice the moon in our sky.

Bathed in high energy ultraviolet radiation
on the surface, the planets need an ozone layer
to protect them, shield from biofluorence.

Early Earth did not have an ozone layer.
Life can shelter underground or in ocean.
Later-launched, space telescopes hope to see methane.

This Trappist-1 system in constellation Aquarius
has rocky, terrestrial planets, maybe water.
If tidally-locked, one side of the planets faces sun.

Life could exist there, if thrived releases gases.
Chemical analysis should indicate life, maybe
similar to what we have on Earth. Unsure until we go.

The ultracool sun is red and shines like twilight.
All seven planets huddle close–like if all our planets
orbited between Mercury and our sun.

With current technology a one-way trip
would take about 100,000 years.
By then we probably could get there quicker.

Astronomers have confirmed 3,600 exoplanets
since 1990s. Four dozen in habitable zone.
18 approximately the size of Earth.

Astronomers are broadening their scope.
Tiny, cold stars like Trappist-1 were shunned
by exo-planet hunters. Now they take another look.

> *The discovery gives us a hint that finding a second Earth is not just a matter of*
> *if, but when and addresses the age-old question of "Are we alone out there?"*
> Thomas Zurbuchen

Another Life-Possible Planet

The latest Goldilocks combination for life,
not so hot and not so cold,
and not so far away planet
is called LHS 1140b in Cetus constellation.

It is the fifth possible planet
outside our solar system revealed
in less than a year, relatively near Earth.
We are feeling less alone.

Rocky planets in a habitable zone
are considered our best bet
to find evidence of some form of life-
maybe microscopic, not too physical?

Astronomers have identified 52
potentially habitable planets
and more than 3,600 planets
outside our solar system–so far.

The latest–LHS 1140b is big--
near the size limit for rocky planets.
40% wider than Earth, 6.6 times our mass.
Gravitational pull three times stronger.

Humans would be really heavy weights
lugging around many more pounds.
It is 39 light years or 230 trillion miles away
so I doubt I will visit. I can add pounds here.

Recently the discovery of seven mostly
Earth-sized planets in a habitable zone
circling a star called Trappist-1
was found in a different direction.

Planets are popping up like popcorn.
Maybe one might not want the invasion of privacy.
They are counting on our lack of access
and rudimentary science to protect them.

Gaga Over Gliese 1132b

Every time scientists discover
a possible planet for us to escape
to when we need to exit Earth they extol
its potentially life-bearing characteristics.

Gliese 1132b is an Earth-like exoplanet
39 light years away–an alien world maybe
capable of hosting life—except
we do not have the capability to go there.

This small, rocky planet 1.4 times
the size of Earth has an atmosphere
and orbits a dim M dwarf (red dwarf).
About one-quarter our sun's radius.

This super-Earth spotted by telescope in Chile,
by the transit method–when a planet
crosses its star and blocks starlight.
They can measure it.

Gliese 1132b- think I'll call it G-B,
has 19 times more stellar radiation
than Earth. Surface temperature 620 degrees
fahrenheit is not considered habitable.

G-B might be the first low mass super-Earth
with detectable atmosphere close to Earth's radius,
but I'm not sure it would be a great choice
for our apocalyptic migration–if we could get there.

The cosmic diversity we find is splendiferous.
We can appreciate the creative grandeur,
but we have a place to be and other beings
might prefer to live their lives elsewhere--

without us. We can invade their privacy
by peering at them, someday perhaps
see them–or perhaps they dwell
in a dimension we cannot perceive.

Perhaps some alien born-that-way beings
are watching us–not gaga but aghast
hoping we get our act together
so we don't come knocking their home.

Fly By?

Exoplanets are mysterious.
Our scientists are curious.
Landscapes we can't imagine,
elude to our chagrin.
Millions out there.
We're not aware
if life forms
conform
norms.
What
if hot
or robot
or strange beings
we are not yet seeing?
And we must face the fact
if we manage to contact
in a distant, far away future–
might not like our violent culture.

Cassini Takes the Plunge

Cassini arrived at Saturn in 2004
to study its 62 known moons
and Saturn's rings.

Moon Titan resembles Earth
they think and Enceladus has oceans
shooting ice particles into space.

To avoid contaminating Enceladus
with Cassini's Earth microbes, Cassini's
grand finale will plunge into Saturn.

Cassini travels 70,000 miles per hour
and hopes to take 22 dives into the rings
unscathed before suicide into Saturn.

Are the rings 4.6 billion years old like Saturn?
Are they later shredded moons or comets?
What are their age and composition?

As Cassini careens around Saturn's
rings and moon—do they know
what seen or unseen beings dwell there?

Maybe Saturn does not want
to be probed and poked. Like Gaia
all has energy and consciousness, some say.

As we intrude into space to fulfill
our curious quests, do we come in peace
or to plunder resources, find safe haven?

Black Hole Binges

1.8 billion light-years from Earth
in a small galaxy from afar,
for over a decade a black hole
binges and devours a dying star.

Since 1990s scientists
observed this food fest,
a feeding frenzy since 2005,
by x-ray telescopes's test.

This monstrous munching
of a star twice as heavy as sun
should taper off in another decade.
Meanwhile it's chewing's not done.

Apparently black holes
like stars well-done, cook
them millions of degrees,
gobble up all they took.

The multiverse is filled with black holes.
But most seem to have year-long binges.
The Milky Way has a central black hole.
Earth lingers on galactic fringes.

Someday it might be time for us
to spiral into a black hole maw.
Until then while cosmos' still stellar,
I'll gape at space with awe.

Expansion

It is useful to live a more clear and balanced life. But overall, the Universe doesn't care about your habits. The Universe cares about your expansion. Sara Wiseman

Well, my weight is expanding with the universe
which is part of a bubbling brane multiverse.
Suppose my smidgeon situation could be worse.

I am trying to raise my frequency,
live more or less with decency,
eat dark chocolate less frequently.

Some say we are star stuff
and just as we are is enough
even when times are tough.

Not sure how I am accountable,
understanding seems insurmountable,
in this dual reality: an illusion or a fable?

This galaxy spins away from others,
not sure if this expansion bothers,
any cosmic mothers and brothers.

I am just a curious, omnivorous ort
trying to comprehend, create and sort
until time to multi-dimensionally transport.

Our expansion of heart/mind
with universe, we could find
what cosmic essences would bind.

Cosmical

Twinkle toes,
wrinkle nose,
no one knows
how life flows,
cosmic glows?

Neophyte,
I delight
seeking light
to ignite
to unite.

Optimist
I insist
we resist
pessimist
to exist.

Magical,
mystical
optimal
corporal
miracle.

We explore.
Can't ignore
to adore
or deplore?
Omnivore?

So meanwhile
seek my style,
search awhile,
an erstwhile
cosmosphile.

Gifts of Gaia

Snowflake 2007

There are two ways to live.
We can live as if nothing is a miracle,
you can live as if everything is a miracle.

Albert Einstein

Looking Out

I am amazed by all forms of wildlife...
from space you can see that Earth
is beautiful, fragile and interconnected.
Leland Melvin, Astronaut

From space we look
so beautiful,
fragile, interconnected.
Polluted sky
obscures space view, dims lights.
Disputable
or irrefutable–
improve or die.

Following the Moon

At a reading by poet Ellen Bass
in the university library, I could see the moon
peering high in the tall glass windows.

The stormy sky darkened as she spoke,
clouds whisked patchy moon-glow.
Shadows obscured the moonscape.

Much as I admire Bass' poetry,
my head would tilt toward the moon,
watch the moon patterns, passing light and dark.

My ears heard poetry, my eyes moonlight.
By question and answer period
the moon had traveled behind wall.

I was drawn to look and listen to her,
hair moon-gray, blue-sky shirt,
mouth open like woman-in-the-moon.

Her fan since her anthology *No More Masks*,
gave women, We'moon, a voice in the 1970s.
As the moon hid tonight, Bass-light continued to shine.

Pink Moon

The first full moon in April
is called the Pink Moon
after all the pink wildflowers.

I would like to see a blushing moon,
or flushing with empowerment
like the pink hats in the Women's March.

But I actually prefer a Blue Moon
for blue is my favorite color–any shade.
Once-in-a-Blue-Moon opens opportunities.

Orange harvest moons, stark white
and grayish moons shape shift, eclipse
as well as change hues and cloud-shadows.

Exotic moons on exo-planets--
ice gushers, ring-orbiters in Milky Way,
lure myths of lovers and aliens.

I moon-watch comfortably
sitting or gaze through a telescope,
stare moonstruck pulling down the shade.

Cloud-Watcher

Clouds
designing
skyscape and our mood.
Sunrise, sunset frame our day.
Blurry, slurry, colorful, gray
changing patterns lure
us to look
up.

Hole-Punch Clouds

Jets hole-punch clouds,
clouds of altocumulus--
altocumulus or cirrocumulus layers,
layers jets have to punch through,
through a collaboration of humans and nature,
nature socked again into these clouds,
clouds also called fallstreak holes,
holes punctured to form big gaps,
gaps gored by our pugnacious jets.

Too Cold

Too cold
to exercise,
wrap up head and torso.
I'll watch snowfall blanching yard white
like cloud-landing, softening surfaces,
rounding edges, wind-swirled mounds–
inviting me to explore.
I'll stay warm. It's
too cold.

Winter Wonder

Sun glistens ice-shine
lifts down mood of mine
today.

Winter's cold design
shivers warmth's decline
away.

New Year's hopes combine
see futures incline,
dismay.

Can't let thoughts resign–
dull, whimper, whine,
betray.

Does weather define?
Open or confine?
Or sway?

Seek the crystalline
for thoughts underline
our stay.

Snowflakes

Every crystal was a masterpiece of design and no one design was ever repeated.
When a snowflake melted, that design was forever lost....I became possessed with a
great desire to show people something of this wonderful loveliness. Wilson Bentley

Wilson Bentley photographed snowflakes'
crystalline structure before they turned into vapor.
500 images are in the Smithsonian.

I am no statistician, but I can't believe
each fleeting snowflake ever to fall on Earth
was one of a kind–no repeats, none identical?

These photographs helped scientists discover
more about the atomic structure of water,
how weather and conditions effect how flakes grow.

How wonderful sacred geometry and art,
even in microscopic sizes exists abundantly!
I am content knowing they are beautiful.

Over the years I have cut paper snowflakes–
sometimes not even white. I struggle
getting one lacy flake to look graceful.

Bentley was a photomicrography pioneer.
To go tiny and study tiny is still trending.
In the multiverse- All absorbs the big and small.

Hail February

Hail bounces on wintry green grass,
leaps from battered branches.
Street blanches, pebbled white. Skylight pelted
leaving splotches on glass.
Writers sit inside and write- we're
melted.

Usually it is rain most days–
quiet, nourishing sound.
Now hail's bobbing around, popping resounds
not our common displays.
Hail's spritely dance on whitened ground–
astounds.

Tunneling Trees
Pioneer Cabin sequoia in California Calaveras Big Trees State Park toppled
January 7, 2017.

Despite being gouged in 1880
to allow horses and cars
to drive through its tunnel--
in an over 1,000 year old trunk,
Pioneer Cabin stood tall
greeting tourists
and inhaling fumes.

But in 2017 a powerful winter storm
ripped out its shallow roots
and shattered it
when it hit the ground.
Pioneer Cabin was one
of 137 living tunnels to greet visitors.
Now some logs live lying
on their side or dead.

In 1964 my husband and I
with our eldest toddler son
stopped and visited
these living tunnels,
but since we had a travel trailer
we could not fit through the gaping maw.

Inside a fallen, hollowed tree
my son and I peered up
through a bark hole–
a natural skylight, in awe
of these trees' gigantic beauty,
in a spotlight surrounded by shadow.

In 1982 our son was killed
in a truck/bike accident.
On a hill we planted a madrona
and scattered his ashes.
The tree grew for decades.
We witnessed its growth
on many visits. Until,
lovers carved their initials too deep
and the tree died. An offshoot thrives.

Back to 2017 I remember these trees
I associate with my son
shelters for light,
shards of our hearts.

Holly Tree in Winter

snow-scabs cling
        to rough bark

snow-cotton-puffs clot
        on shiny leaves

snow-bandages blot
        blood-ish berries

Bug Battles

My walker squished an elongated bug in the bathroom--
splat black under the yellow tennis ball on one leg.
Was my action intentional? Could I have swerved?

There are billions of bugs and billions of people
all here to live out multitudinous destinies?
How much control over how, who dies and when?

We set up toxic tents for moths, swat flies,
step on ants, poison bugs–who put us in control?
So much for cooperation and sharing.

This morning's victim will sluff off
as I scuff across the floor. I will not tilt
the walker to check when it is gone.

The walker is four-legged pushed by two-legged.
Does legged-ness or size decide who is dominant?
Is there some protocol for species interaction?

Perhaps I need to think how much killing
is necessary in the insect community,
as well as witness for peace for all.

Bugged
Earthweek: Diary of a Changing World Week ending February 10, 2017

LED streetlights despite significant
energy saving capabilities, harm
insects and wildlife. Artificial light
of streetlights attracts beetles and spiders,
increasing damage to vegetation
and other species. Dim the lights.

Hordes of crop-destroying,
army worm caterpillars are spreading
rapidly across Africa and could invade
Asia and the Mediterranean–a major threat
to agricultural trade. They munch maize,
rice, soybean, pasture grass and potato.

In Australia antidote supplies are low
for the funnel-web spider whose bite
is deadly. Residents are urged
to capture these arachnids and deliver them
to experts, so the venom can be extracted
for treatment. Spiders like hot summers.

Climate is bugging Pakistan –earthquakes.
Earth movements in Turkey, Italy, Papua,
islands in the Caribbean and Columbia.
Desert chill record just above freezing in Qatar.
In Sumatra, the Sinabung volcano
spewed ash requiring face masks.

Meanwhile in Washington D.C.
someone bugs the White House with leaks, fake news.
Russian hacking, bugging computers--un-swat.
The President bugs the world with tweets, lies,
incompetent cabinet appointments, ban on immigrants,
harsh executive orders, alternative facts–bugaboos.

Goat Yoga

Goat yoga combines a one-hour yoga session with the animal-therapy of social mini-goats that wander around and interact with the class. Nathan Brutell

Rolling in the hay
with a trip of goats
is a new yoga way
to float their boats.
      It's popularity is a puzzle.
      Yoga for a goat nuzzle?

With a trip of goats
they practice their poses.
While they are feeling their oats,
they're nudged by goat noses.
      As you smell the grass, for the class,
      you've entered the goat world alas.

Is the new yoga way
to use goats to heal?
Goat's antics leap stress away,
their cuddles are goat's appeal.
      With yoga mat and open mind,
      a reduction in negativity you'll find.

To float their boats
they flow on calming seas.
As the yoga novelty floats
they relieve their disease.
      The rollicking goats make them smile.
      They forget their troubles for awhile.

It's popularity is a puzzle,
from Oregon's No Regrets farm start.
Now in global spotlight, the buzz'ill
let more people to take part.
      Horses too big. Dogs get runny.
      Goats better size, than a bunny.

Yoga for a goat nuzzle
adds a new tactile dimension.
Social media's spread doesn't muzzle
delight in goat snuggle's intention.
      Enjoy a Goat Happy Hour.
      Sweat, then sing in the shower.

Stranded Whales in New Zealand

Along Farewell Spit at the tip of the South Island,
in two mass strandings, 650 pilot whales beached.
350 whales died. 100 whales were refloated by volunteers,
200 whales swam away unassisted.

Hundreds of volunteers from farmers to tourists
doused the whales with buckets of water
to keep them cool, trying to refloat them.
The first group of 400 beached whales were found dead.

The volunteers sang songs to them,
gave them each a name, treating them
like the kindred spirits they are. Hopefully
the marine mammal's strandings are over.

These strandings happen due to unknown causes--
disoriented? Sick? Directional malfunctions?
What about the seismic booms from oil searchers
leaving sea creatures deaf, bloodied, starving?

Immigrants of all species washed up on shores,
due to climate change, political chaos, war,
will volunteers be compassionate or try to refloat them
back to devastated areas–unassisted, beached.

Seascape

Patches of sunlight patterns glisten on the ocean.
Swatches of light through cloud pockets sparkle the sea.
Prancing down the cliff path to the sand,
dancing light on waves dazzles the hikers.

Lurking deep the threatened living creatures,
murking in the depths our waste debris devours.
Surface perception all is glittery, deceptive.
Embrace momentary beauty whenever seen.

Below acid brew bleaches reefs elsewhere
but know toxic stew effects sea life here.
Gazing at the rippling sun-puckered sunset
raises questions what to do before all's darkened.

PCBs Pollute the Seas

PCBs found down in the deepest depths of the sea.
The Mariana and Kermadec trenches--
two of the deepest ocean chasms
have "extraordinary levels "of PCBs.

Industrial pollution now in once pristine places.
Contaminants sink and enter marine environments.
Of about 1.3 million tons of PCBs produced,
38 percent still reside in coastal sediment.

Banned in the 1970s, PCBs do not degrade
naturally and remain for decades bonding
with bits of plastic and organic debris–transported
by air, soil, coastal waters–even found in the Arctic.

Amphipods–tiny shrimp-like creatures
ingest contaminants in ocean's hadal zone
3.7 to 6.8 miles deep. Stored in their fat,
Amphipods spread PCBs up the food chain when eaten.

Twelve animals collected were contaminated
regardless of trench depth, trench or species.
Elevated concentrations of contaminates found
even had flame retardant. PCBs are toxic.

The Mariana Trench is the most contaminated--
near to industrialized regions and beneath
Great Pacific Garbage Patch. Plastic debris,
contaminated dead animals sink. Amphipods devour.

PCBs devastate hormonal, immune
and reproductive systems. The deep sea
is more connected to the surface than people think.
Pollutants effect physiology and ecosystems adversely.

Scientists continue to collect data, evidence
of PCB pollution. Once they were used in transformers,
capacitors, electrical devices before banned.
But PCB residue remains, destroying environments.

Water Pressure

Hydrogen is transformative in several ways.
Scientists pressured it so intensely
they created a new element- metal hydrogen.
In other states it has so much to do.

Now scientists say water inside the Earth
is made by pressure between quartz
and liquid hydrogen in the mantle
between core and crust.

A hidden ocean as large as oceans
we can see, locked up inside the Earth?
The pressure could trigger earthquakes
and life-sustaining volcanoes.

We need this store of water
for geodynamic activity of volcanoes
which generate soil
and sustain life on the planet.

They have found rare diamonds
containing ringwoodite,
water-rich, formed by water pressure.
Diamond mines- allowed to go further?

We thought our water came
from icy comets billions of years ago.
But now think water born inside
the Earth itself!

With our new technology
we need to be careful
not to dig too deep.
Water is found 620 miles below the surface.

We were counting on tunneling deep
for nuclear dumps which could
contaminate this water, un-stabilize.
Just think if the inner ocean joined outer!

Inner Earth civilization theories might drown.
How far we can plunge into the planet, alter?
We can't live without water
no matter where we find it.

Earth Day Egg

The night after Earth Day
I dreamed I was given a large egg--
a re-gifted Easter egg?

As I gazed at the egg,
it cracked open. Four fluffy,
yellow chicks emerge.

I cupped my arms with the chicks,
and wondered what I was
to do with them. Gift them?

Our daughter had cats.
Our son had dogs. Friends had pets.
We have no pets. So I guess I'm the hen.

I knew I should find a soft, warm spot
for them, perhaps some food soon.
I would not eat a pet- so cuddly and cute.

As I pondered their fate,
they flit to the window sill,
dancing in pink tutus.

I awoke with images of chubby chicks
celebrating thousands of marchers
in the global March for Science that day?

Pipelines

Energy companies ramp up
new pipelines to move natural gas glut
        to refineries and export terminals.

Native Americans and environmental activists
resisted Dakota Access Pipeline
        to protect their land and water.

In Pennsylvania fracking shale
created an over-supply of natural gas, depressing
        prices, hampering economic development.

Yet they keep fracking, grabbing land,
laying pipes in Pennsylvania where
        they have 12,000 miles of oil and gas pipelines.

Like coal trains our resources
are shipped overseas, endangering our land,
        jobs becoming obsolete, robotic.

The nation is tunneled with pipelines,
wormholes for flow of gas and oil.
        Eminent domain takes land it can't buy.

New pipelines use advanced coatings,
have better and safer engineering than older lines
        supporters say–provide plastics and chemical jobs.

When will we turn to renewable energy,
clean jobs, environmentally sustainable?
        How can residents protect their land?

When the pipes break, oil and gas leak,
the water's contaminated, the land's scarred,
        how do we defend need and greed?

Resistance to the pipeline network broadens
as people weigh benefits and costs.
        Delay the pipe for pipe dreams.

How to Dispose of Nuclear Waste?

Nuclear fuel remains radioactive thousands of years.
Global stockpiles of spent nuclear fuel balloons.
Political backlash and backyard dump fears.
Some disposal places seek economic boons.
> Where do we put waste storage?
> We can't spill toxic porridge!

Global stockpiles of spent nuclear fuel balloons.
Billions of taxpayers and companies bear cost,
until final waste storage problem tightly cocoons.
All of humanity could be lost.
> Several countries dig underground tombs.
> The chance of leakage, accident looms.

Political backlash and backyard dump fears,
some of the hurdles, lack resolution.
But the Finns are willing it appears.
Think they have the technological solution.
> Tunnel system 100 stories underground.
> What if burial chamber in future found?

Some disposal places seek economic boon.
Olkiluoto Island offered Finnish land.
Activists wanted more studies–and soon
trying to know risks, help locals understand.
> Even hardest bedrock will be cracked,
> leak into groundwater, to Baltic Sea tracked.

Where do we put waste storage?
Onkalo is constructing an underground tomb.
How to protect those in a future age?
Leaving the nuclear problem to loom.
> How to deal with waste impacts society,
> fills us with world-wide anxiety.

We can't spill toxic porridge!
We have discovered an inner-earth sea.
Some obstacles we cannot bridge.
We can't spoon it all up, eventually.
> Deep-in-the-earth burials the safest way?
> Future generations may have to pay.

Freeganism

Freeganism is the practice and technology of limited participation in the
conventional economy and minimal consumption of resources, particularly
through recovering wasted goods like food...they avoid buying anything as an
act of protest against the food system...distinguished by their association with
anti-consumerist and anti-capitalist ideology and their engagement in
alternative living strategies such as voluntary unemployment, squatting
abandoned buildings and guerilla gardening in unoccupied park. Wikipedia

With the wealth inequities top 1% over 99%
one wonders how much Freeganism is voluntary.
In recessions and depressions it's a survival skill.
Their anti-waste actions might be necessary.

Dumpster diving is one way of rummaging--
fast food and grocery discards to consumers directly,
reduces waste, could feed many more
if could develop process to distribute correctly.

Furniture left at curb for the taking.
Shelter in unused, uninhabited places.
Food banks and food drops to forage,
we need more feeding and sleeping places.

Like Diggers and Black Panthers
caring and resource sharing,
volunteers at shelters, community gardens,
helping others with too few preparing.

Urban and wild foraging might face more demand,
than can be handled environmentally.
Healthcare access and educational opportunities,
recycling, squatting could increase incrementally.

Concerns about sanitation, poaching property,
legal, cultural and stigma issues fraught.
Food Not Bombs and Feedback groups help cause,
to give from the haves to the have nots.

We live in a very inequitable time,
gated communities, sub-urbanization,
low wages, high rents and prices,
away from the farm and more urbanization.

Some Freegans connect with "back to the landers"
but how much land is available for pioneering?
Living off the grid, foraging commercial dumpster discards--
new hunting and gathering commandeering.

Homeless individuals and families
is a world-wide circumstance.
Refugee camps, immigration shifts
a measure how our well-being will advance?

Some are Freegans for amusement, religious reasons,
but despite convictions it shows societal breakdown.
Access must change to serve more people.
Think of all the billions as problems compound.

Climate change and economic upheavals,
indicate Freeganism is here to stay.
If we could work together globally
we might develop in a safe, peaceful way.

Don't Shade Our Shine

The Doomsday Clock has moved:
two minutes-thirty seconds to midnight.
Time's running out for this planet we've loved.
Can we act to reverse this plight?
    Blue cloudy marble shining bright
    glows artificial light at night.

Two minutes-thirty seconds to midnight:
the disaster hand clicks.
Will end be cosmic or by human rite?
Global catastrophe as time ticks?
    All worry about a miscue.
    Understanding options are few.

Time's running out for this planet we've loved.
Gaia gasps, spews liquid and gas,
watches her surface dug and shoved.
Yet Gaia should remain, without people, alas.
    Maybe new tenants will be seeded,
    after the dangers have receded?

Can we act to reverse this plight?
Perhaps we face forces we can't overcome?
Or lose some nonviolent fight?
Would alien intervention be welcome?
    Will energy be re-arranged? Our consciousness purged?
    Will we be temporarily deranged as a new reality surged?

Blue cloudy marble shining bright
seen from near-Earth neighborhood,
glistening with telescope and satellite--
will we just blip out for good?
    Is a thing of beauty a joy forever?
    End it on purpose? Hopefully never.

Glows artificial light at night,
blurs the stars in polluted air.
Star light, star bright
not seen from Earth tonight?
    Shades of darkness will envelop
    if all shades of humans don't develop.

Snowflake Blues

Only when the last tree has died and the last river has been poisoned and the last fish has been caught will we realize that we can not eat money.   Chief Seattle

Snowflakes
   can melt hearts
when progress makes
   some re-starts.
 Their liberal minds
   seek more counterparts.
 Seattle reminds:
fight as long as it takes.

Ancient Mysteries

Tut

All things quiver with the past.

Doug Stone

Lost Continents

The Island of Mauritius sits
on sunken continent which fits
the way early continents did splits.

Zircon crystals 3 billion years old
have been found there I've been told.
But Mauritius is only 8 million years old.

Small continent about size of Madagascar
when shifted from Madagascar to India far
from where they now are.

Pieces of old continents found near Iceland
and off Western Australia's land.
Searching deep ocean for continents planned.

All continents shift over time.
Part of cosmic plan of Prime
Mover? Some force sublime?

Some say universe is a hologram.
Some energy designs who I am.
All part of some cryptogram?

Others say we are a simulation,
played by superintellience's contemplation,
creating a game from our situation.

All has energy and consciousness somehow?
Maybe interstellar clouds of electrons have know-how,
sparked from superintelligence controllers to grow?

Some superintelligence controls cosmic tests,
multiple, parallel multiversal contests?
Each created a place where its energy crests?

A fine structural constant controls how atoms
are put together so right parameter hums
and they can experiment with outcomes?

If we are a simulation we must
be in one that lasts so we can trust
our existence might not just bust.

Someday our microchips could power
a simulation of universe, then we could shower
our complex creation higher and make continents lower.

Without the right game rules we can't exist.
Planets and stars would not persist
with mysteries we can't resist.

Land masses go up and down, Lemuria? Mu?
Flood wipe outs and then Atlantis too?
Lots more exploration into particle zoo.

Zealandia–Recently Discovered Continent

...a fair consensus in the scientific community in favor of its existence...It's
pretty clear that that whole area is not part of the ocean. It's got all the
hallmarks of a continent...It was all once part of a huge continent that's all
broken up into little pieces of the puzzle.   Barry Kohn

Geologists argued for Zealandia for over 20 years.
The continent was hidden in plain sight it appears.
Now scientific consensus and data --clears.

A new continent submerged in the SW Pacific
a vast, continuous expanse of continental crust–terrific,
centers in New Zealand to be specific.

Zealandia covers 1.9m square miles.
94% underwater, meanwhile
evidence continues to pile.

Zealandia sunk between 60-85 million years ago--
broke away from Gondwana land mass, they know
Australia was part of it. Scientists say so.

New Caledonia, New Zealand,
Lord Howe Island group, Norfolk Island,
Reefs Elizabeth and Middleton reefs in this land.

Zealand is 7th and smallest continent:
after Eurasia, Africa, North America, (then went)
South America, Antarctica and Australia (full content)?

They dredged rock clearly continental crust,
more data over decades prove Zealandia must
be a continent with evidence scientists trust.

I was hoping they found Lemuria or Mu,
or added data for the Atlantis hullaballoo.
Those are myths I hope someday prove true.

Antikythera Mechanism

Near an island between Peloponnese and Crete
Greek divers found a 2,000 year old ship wreck
with a portable cosmos almost complete.
Years before scientists could check.
      Among biggest ancient Greek sculptural hoard
      Antikythera Mechanism was once on board.

Greek divers found a 2,000 year old ship wreck
with oopart gizmo, geared like computer.
In 1900 scientists were not sufficiently high tech
to see inside and explore this concept-transmuter.
      A fragile slab of corroded metal was important artifact--
      perhaps the first analog computer found in fact.

With a portable cosmos almost complete
to keep a calendar, track heavenly bodies, eclipses--
a scientific breakthrough-- its discovery could compete
with opening pyramids, finding atomic bombs, it implies ellipses.
      In 1970 x-ray images glimpse hidden gears,
      and inscriptions. More insight appears.

Years before scientists could check,
fragments stashed in cigar boxes lingered.
Scholars barely knew it existed, no spec
of this remarkable creation was fingered.
      Now they believe it might be a teaching aid
      or to compute data, or for predictions made.

Among biggest ancient Greek sculptural hoard
which included bronze statue "Antikythera Youth"--
it was one of top ten archeological discoveries explored
beside bones of technician who might know its truth.
      Today we can marvel at our clever, ancient kin
      despite their inefficient gearwork flawed within.

Antikythera Mechanism was once on board--
a treasure which an interdisciplinary team decoded.
This astronomical tool strikes a resonant chord,
its ingenuity and knowledge time has not eroded.
      With our portable screens, telescopes on sky
      we can see the cosmos-- but we still ask why.

Microbial Cave Dwellers

It's simply another illustration of just how completely tough Earth life is.
Penelope Boston

In a Mexican cave called both fairyland and hell,
50,000 years old life in crystals dwell.
Cave is hot and beautiful, scientists tell.

Weird Naica cave system is so hot,
scientists wear cheap space suits to spot
life forms and prevent contamination's onslaught.

40 different strains of microbes confound.
Even some strange viruses were found.
Nearest relative 10% different. Facts compound.

Microbes can survive in extremely punishing conditions,
evolve even in crystals with many renditions,
exist living on minerals-- iron, manganese editions.

Naica caves in an abandoned lead and zinc mine,
before drilling was completely cut-off and pristine
with vast, cathedral, iron walls covered –crystalline.

Scientists need ice packs to cool,
cave conditions can be cruel,
curiosity is their fuel.

Some microbes half a million years old are alive.
Some trapped in ice and salt still survive.
Some in crystal will revive.

Microbe studies in the United States and Ukraine
and elsewhere find they eat copper sulfate–insane.
Indestructible like the tardigrade, they remain.

Life on Earth can be tough for us.
Comebacks from extinction–miraculous.
Next time could be disastrous.

If people are gone, microbes could rebuild.
Minerals they can continue to gild.
Their elemental, earthly mission instilled.

For eons people and microbes shared caves,
no matter how planet behaves.
Both groups could end up in cosmic enclaves.

Swimming Toward a Branch of our Family Tree

Scientists found a bag-like sea creature
they claim was our oldest known ancestor,
a fossil found in China claimed as the earliest
evolutionary step which lead to humans.

Saccorhytus Coronarius is a millimeter sea sack
from 540 million years ago, predating other deuterostomes--
a bi-lateral creature wriggling in mud, living
between grains of sand, with a big mouth, no anus.

Really ugly. Like a green space helmet
with large, gaping, dark mouth surrounded
by three rings of golden dots and gold pimples.
Like a green alien skull detached from its body.

Perhaps this creature did belong to a group
which encompassed many other groups
including vertebrates, but it took awhile
to swim to shore and add some limbs.

Perhaps modern human species,
honed from many branches on our family tree
has such ancient DNA still floating at sea,
planning to join other species climbing our tree.

Human Hybrids

Dem bone dem bones, dem dry bones
Dem bones, dem bones, dem dry bones
Den bones, dem bones, dem dry bones
Now shake dem skeleton bones...
    J. Rosomond Johnson

A pair of newly found partial skulls
located in China's Henan province,
unseen before in hominid fossil chronicle.
Both human and Neanderthal features convince
      scientist have discovered a hybrid human,
      living long before we thought humans began.

Located in China's Henan province
inhabited 105,000 to 125,000 years ago,
it has been a long time since
these archaic ancestors let us know.
      Quartz blades, good hunters from bones near
      of horses, cattle, wooly rhinoceros, giant deer.

Unseen before in hominid fossil chronicle
like Denisovans from a Siberian cave,
these Chinese bones puzzle. Science culls
these "mosaic" featured skulls. They have
      human broad and flat brainpan
      and Neanderthal ear canals, enlarged back skull–not human.

Both human and Neanderthal features convince
Denisovans related for also have both DNA.
Taken from finger bone and tooth evidence.
Human hybrids exist to this day.
      New archaic humans survived in East Asia,
      somehow preserved through millennia.

Scientists have discovered a human hybrid
to help fill in the gaps, branches of family tree.
There are many ways to be hominid,
as we try to understand the mystery.
      But what causes this evolution
      and is that the only solution?

Living long before we thought humans began,
life teamed, inhabiting many forms.
Hybrids part of following some cosmic plan?
Sentience may have dwelled within many norms.
Were they seeded after an extinction?
Will our species have the same distinction?

Dem bones, dem bones just found
Dem bones, dem bones confound
Dem bones, dem bones dumbfound
Dem bones are really profound.

Chinese Tomb Mates

An ancient tomb holds a general and princess wife
buried on March 18, 564. They surrounded themselves
with 105 items, mostly pottery figurines,
of warriors, camels, oxcarts and drummers.
Still colorful, the tallest figurine was 22 inches.

A sandstone inscription describes the life
of Zhao Xin and his wife Princess Nee Liu
and when they were buried together.
"On the 290 day of the second moon of the third year
of the Heqing period." Helpful, long-lasting tombstone.

Zhao Xin held posts as a general and at times
a governor in different parts of China,
serving the rulers of the Northern Qi dynasty,
which controlled northern China 550-577.
His final post was as general at Huangniu Town.

Zhao Xin lead his garrison of men to victory in battle.
"A thousand men lost their souls; he disposed
of the Yi barbarians and exterminated the enemy,
and the public flocked to him." says the inscription.
He died at 67 while still general of the garrison.

The inscription described Princess Nee Liu:
"by nature, she was modest and humble,
and sincerity and filial piety were her roots.
Her accommodating nature was clear,
her behavior respectful and chaste."

The inscription does not say why they were buried
at the same time. Bone analysis not been published yet.
The tomb was found in a mountain location near
modern day Taiyuan city, in the eastern foothills
of the Xishan Mountains on west bank of Fenhe River.

The inscription says: if the mountain peak's roots
are firm, it can contend in height with Heaven and Earth;
deep and brilliant, solid and bright, it speeds
far away along with the Sun and Moon; civil and martial
seek each other, and so men are naturally there.

Archaeologists found 69 other tombs in the cemetery.
With new technology we can find ancient burials
of various types all over the world, many honoring the dead.
Most not with such elaborate inscriptions as this couple.
Modern tombstones usually have brief dates, short epitaphs.

These tomb mates inscribed their obituary
and like Egyptians brought along cherished items.
Today's obituaries are also flattering, all people's assets
and achievements, ignoring flaws and failures.
Perhaps good deeds are more worth remembering.

On the Internet our information could last quite a while,
until a solar flare, nuclear holocaust, meteorite blast
causes our extinction-- and then perhaps no one could read it.
All the dead above and below ground–could be cremated.
Ashes blowing in the polluted air. Spirits soaring into space.

Mysteries at Two Henges

In the Neolithic settlement of Durrington Walls,
Brits dwelled between henges of wood and stone.
Folks 4500 BC had solstice protocols
in their Stone Age life style mostly unknown.
      Stonehenge honored spirits of the dead?
      Woodhenge celebrated life's renewal instead?

Brits dwelled between henges of wood and stone
with Stonehenge Cursus as a dividing line
between henges both marvels of their own,
until metal brought henges into decline.
      Were henges built to increase fertility,
      by stone workers and engineers with ability?

Folks 4500 BC had solstice protocols,
watched solstice sun between poles of wood
or sun-slit between tall stone slab-walls,
bringing celebrations to their neighborhood.
      Their practices involve investigations,
      and speculations over many generations.

In their Stone Age life style mostly unknown
they organized large scale cooperation,
built henges with antler bone,
places for worship and celebration?
      People would parade between the two
      henges down a wide, grand avenue.

Stonehenge honored spirits of the dead?
Respect ancestors, stone symbolizes eternity?
Cremations washed into river instead,
but sun-worship, ashes remain in modernity.
      Stonehenge a place to face life cycle?
      Return of sun considered a miracle?

Woodhenge celebrated life's renewal instead?
Waste and rubbish there show feasting excessive.
Place to procreate, get drunk, forget dread?
Place to insure fertility so community successive?
      Life and death symbolized by movements of the sun.
      Henges encircled lives with grand vision for everyone.

Handbag Evolution

Ancient carvings and crafts around the world
depict a person, god or mythical being
carrying a handbag similar to present times--
a rounded handle-like top and rectangular bottom
with details varying in texture and pattern.

Throughout time these mysterious handbags,
first seen at the end of the Iron Age
appear as an important if puzzling symbol.
What are they carrying?
How did these handbag images travel globally?

One handbag theory is it represents the cosmos.
Semi-circle: the hemispheric dome of the sky,
the solid square represents Earth.
In ancient cultures from Africa, India to China
a circle is symbol of spirituality,
or non-materiality while square is earth.
A handbag unifies earth and sky,
material with non-material elements of existence.

The handbag motif is found in Gobekli Tepe
in Turkey about 11,000 BC. Purpose unknown.
Butchered bones indicate a sacrifice site.
Walls and pillars have finely carved animals,
gods and mythical creatures. Maybe
they carried handbags with food or items
for their worshiping or gossiping gatherings.

The Assyrians in ancient Iraq 880-859 BC
and the Olmecs in Mesoamerica 1200-400 BC
had a standard handbag measurement in both cultures.
Assyrians said purse contains magic dust.
Olmecs said it contains herbs to get you high.

In Maori myth a hero ascends to home of gods
and returns to Earth with three handbags
of wisdom, like the three handbags found
at Gobekli Tepi. Symbolize worship and
gratitude for divinely inspired knowledge? Aliens?

Egyptian hieroglyphics serve as a home
for gods and goddesses. The straps being
dome poles of a portable tent.
The bottom square is cloth or animal skins
laid across poles like teepee or Asian yurt.
Like a medicine man's healing pouch?

Like pyramids and other sacred geometry
these handbags show ancient cultural connections.
Did ancestors get knowledge from star beings,
creative intuition, or were more connected than we know?
We have learned they really dispersed,
carrying their handbags with them?

Today handbags have migrated to shoulders,
belly packs, backpacks, luggage filled
with whatever the carrier wants to carry.
Combs, cosmetics, computers, cell, candy, clothes,
keys, paper, paper clips, pens, pencils, pills...
My black, adjustable strap handbag
with compartments and zippers transports
the material detritus of my day.

Footprints at Walmadany
James Prince Point, Australia

The Goolarabooloo knew about dinosaur trackways
for millennia through their song cycles.
Part of their creation mythology,
these massive markings show the journey
of a creation being called Marala- the emu man.
Wherever he went he left three-toed tracks,
which we recognize today as meat-eating dinosaurs.

Thousands of twenty-one different types of dinosaurs
lived together at the same time, in same area
over 100 million years ago and left tulip-shaped marks
despite climate changes, continent shifts, asteroid strikes.
Northwestern Australia's Jurassic Park
has the most diverse dinosaur footprint collection
found in the world—fossil evidence from early-Cretaceous.

The markings needed protection when Walmadany
was selected for a natural gas plant.
The Goolarabooloo asked paleontologists
to look at the tracks so the world would know
what sacred and scientific site would be lost.
In 2011 the area became a Natural Heritage site.
The song cycles continue, dinosaurs track through time.

What footprints, trackways, markings
will remain of the Anthropocene?
Will we have scoured other era's legacy?
Will our globs of garbage, plastic waste,
radiation, toxins have wiped out everyone
so whatever is left is unwitnessed?
Will Goolarabooloo song cycles still seek Marala?

Marala was the Lawgiver. He gave this country rules
we need to follow, on how to behave,
keep things in balance in this magical wilderness.
The songlines, pathways, lead through time.
For Gaia, can we pay attention to the markings,
pass on oral histories while creating new stories
and songs preserving, conserving our heritage?

Walmadany Coroborree 2012

We must hold this land. We must hold it for everyone. Paddy Poe

On the night of the blue moon
from sunset to moonrise
people from all around the world,
all races, different countries
came to dance and sing together
on the pristine Kimberly Peninsula coastline
at Walmadany, Australia.

Indigenous law keepers lead songs and dances
to the beat of wooden sticks
to celebrate holding the land
from eco-cide from mining,
to keep fish from poisoning,
from desecrating burials
near protected dinosaur tracks.
Modern feet joining ancient footprints
to hold this land for all of us.

Runes

The Runes are one of the world's greatest spiritual resources. They speak to us from the depth of our own hearts. Marianne Williamson

R. Buckminster Fuller called The Book Of Runes
a midwife for the rebirth of an ancient oracle.
For practical decision making- a self-help tool,
an over thousand year old tradition, a modern miracle?

I have a set of Viking runic stones to consult.
Book signed by author Ralph H. Blum,
dedicated to anthropologist Margaret Mead.
I face a question that makes me glum.

"Why do we have to have Donald Trump in power?"
I reached for a rune stone in a gray sack,
cast the rune of Algiz or protection.
During shifts in life course, accelerate self-change.

Its important not to collapse into your emotions.
With new opportunities and challenges of this rune,
may come trespasses and unwanted influences.
Remain mindful, with right action, stay in tune.

Correct conduct is your only protection.
Don't pull down the veil and escape from life
by denying what is happening. You will progress.
That is your protection from this strife.

Temperance and courtesy are sinews
of this runes' protective powers, but Trump
doesn't drink, yet acts disrespectfully.
We need protection from this chump.

Ancient runes have motifs - icons for protection
inscribed on jewelry, weapons and tools--
potent symbolic meanings and underlying purposes,
divinatory symbolism for magical rules.

Runes for incantations for protections
blessings, curses, replaced by Latin
writing system after 1100 CE when Rome's
colonization did from 150 CE rune writing in.

Do magical echoes survive in these runes?
Modern folks can pull runes for guidance?
These runes are for healing, merciful, do no harm.
Play with possibility for turbulence's subsidence.

Runes are a "mirror for the magic of our Knowing selves",
a means to communicate with knowledge
of our subconscious minds. An oracle points attention
to hidden fears, future motivations to acknowledge.

These elements become absorbed into the choice realm.
Oracles don't absolve you of your responsibility,
but direct your attention to inner choices,
help you to widen future opportunity.

Perhaps some points are relevant and accepted.
Some find consistent appropriateness in each rune.
Random selections can't be explained by science.
They speak of change and growth, ways to attune.

Positive aspects are transparent, transforming,
can help remove blockages for a breakthrough.
The inner seeker-after-truth could help save us
from ourselves and suggest what to do.

This rune draw sets me to thinking what answers
I can find in this dilemma from my mind and heart,
to alleviate pain, division, hatred, greed
that tends to separate and makes us feel apart.

I will write, march, protest dark intentions
wear heart on my sleeve, adorn a safety pin.
Maybe I will draw another rune for suggestions
of other ways I can join nonviolent kin.

Quotidian Discoveries

Quill

So many worlds,
so much to do,
so little done,
such things to be.

Alfred Lord Tennyson

Omens

On a rare sunny March day
I spotted a solitary, white, heart-shaped petal
on the black asphalt parking lot.
No other petals around.
It felt like a message of love.
The heart made me think of unfurled angel wings.

I saw the petal en route to my car with my walker,
after a three-shot attempt at a blood draw at the clinic.
Two punctures in left elbow crease
under one cotton ball and one on my right hand.
Walking with cloudlets under my coat,
somehow I felt a little less sore. Uplifted.

I went to exercise class after several weeks absence
due to an attack of sciatica. My walker
held my rubber band and weights.
A kind near seat mate carried my
weights and bands with hers to the closet.
Another woman stacked my chair.

Then on to massage. I crawled up the stairs.
The previous client had been very cranky.
Though in pain, I try to make her laugh and we have fun.
A black bird–probably a crow–walked along
the roof-line just outside the window.
When I see a close, black bird- I sense my mother.

After lunch I went to play Scrabble with English teachers.
I brought them copies of my latest book.
I was able to get into the house without assistance.
A penny in the car's driver drink cup holder
reminds me my son recently dropped by.
Kindnesses and omens let me feel cared for–by someone.

We went to dinner with friends at a Thai restaurant.
We do not go often, but the owners lived next door
to our son and somehow the waitress saw what I ordered
and remembered it was not what I usually ordered.
If she had not told me, I would have had a meal
I would not have enjoyed very much. We gave her a good tip.

Then the four of us went to a play at the university,
written by a student. It was called Boom. No assigned seats.
To our astonishment four seats had a sign saying
they were reserved for us by name. First row.
There was a space for my wheelchair. Wonderful seats.
All day I noticed little omens– symbols and actions of light.

Red Rooster Year : 2017

This year
look for
up predictions
for
down predictions–
many.

Fire
spews,
earthquakes–
Red Rooster year
disasters?   Hopes?
Any?

The Apathetic Children

They are like Snow White, they just fall away from the world. Elizabeth Hultcrantz

Uppgivenhetssyndrom or Resignation syndrome said to exist only in
Sweden and only among refugees. The patients lost the will to live.

When refugees have been rejected for asylum,
hundreds of children become totally passive,
immobile, withdrawn, mute, unable to eat and drink,
do not react to physical stimulus or pain.
Unconscious, they have lost their will to live.

Most of the children emigrated from former
Soviet and Yugoslav states.
They know only the safety, culture
and language of Sweden.
They can't envision a life elsewhere.

Sweden has been the most compassionate nation.
They have welcomed hundreds of thousands of refugees.
But they cannot all stay. Some are not given asylum.
Swedes signed petitions to keep apathetic children
and other asylum seekers from deportation.

The apathetic children were from "holistic cultures"
where it is "difficult to draw boundaries between
the individual's private sphere and the collective domain".
Children were sacrificing themselves
to save their families from deportation.

Check ups on apathetic children who were deported
on a stretcher, showed they did not fare well.
Swedes try to save and heal those they can,
but the only cure is asylum for the family.
It takes months to recover even when they stay.

Vibrant children become apathetic,
They feel the only country they can have a life
is Sweden. They have no underlying
physical or neurological disease.
This coma is a form of protection

Children filled psychiatric wards.
Mothers barely spoke and stared into darkness.
Blinds were shut. Lights were off --
the children clinging to life to stay.
By their silence they are heard.

Phone of the Wind: Whispers to Lost Families

On a hill in Otsuchi town in northwestern Japan
there is a white phone booth with glass panes
called "Telephone of the Wind."
        Nearby a bell tolls.

A disconnected rotary phone
invites mourners to speak to their loved ones,
their words carried on the wind.
        Nearby the waves crash the shore.

Over 10,000 visitors in six years came to mourn
over 15,000 residents lost in the tsunami
from the 2011 Great East Japan Earthquake.
        Nearby at noon they play an upbeat song.

Men, women and children enter the booth,
speaking of their grief, updating family news,
feeling just by talking it keeps them alive.
        Nearby others overhear whispers.

The documentary allowed me to listen
to the translations of their heartbreak,
as my own lost ones ached my heart.
        Nearby I reach for the remote.

Whispers to the wind by phone or prayer
hope wherever loved ones are, they are happy,
perhaps they are listening.
        Nearby perhaps my loved ones know.

Ringling No More

The circus will not be coming to town.
Ringling Brothers are not bringing in enough
money from dwindling crowds. Expensive to move.
Animal rights law suits deleted elephants.

Cirque du Soleil is the new artistic circus
without animal abuse, tigers whipped into shape,
elephants prodded into unnatural poses,
clowns running about under high-wire acts,
men burst out of canons, noise, popcorn, peanuts-
no side shows exploiting anomalies.

No child will run away to join
the old circus, but may dream
of new Cirque du Soleils.
Plenty of magic in these shows.

In the digital age all ages have their devices
of anytime access to movies, entertainment.
Animal activist groups protect endangered animals.
Would players of Pokeman Go go to a circus tent?
A three-ring circus in any setting
is not as daring as their world.

As a young child, I was invited
by a neighbor to go to the circus.
I said no because the elephants stank.
That day was the Hartford circus fire.
I would have been in the inflamed section.
Still not fond of elephant as a political symbol.

Fire safety improved, but it was many years
before I took my children to a small circus
in our town. I was looking for exits.
Noisy, dirty, lethargic trained animals,
clowns scary not funny. Last hurrah for me.
Cirque du Soleil only since then.

Riding the Bus

In 1950s white, suburban Connecticut
my non-driving mother rode the bus to the city.
Buses were not segregated.
Our town segregated by income
and religion. No races to segregate.
My mother observed other ethnic
communities on her bus excursions
to the city, but did not interact
with them until later in life.

On my school bus, the pale crowd
was mostly well-behaved.
Icky boys collected frogs' eyes
from biology class which
they flickered from fingers
like a pea shooter
to slime the bus...once.
Otherwise just pesky, hair-pulling,
tripping, annoying boy behavior.

I took the bus to the city
to work weekends
at a large department store.
Reliably the bus took me
from the bus stops without incident.
I enjoyed my diverse customers
and friendly passengers.

With the civil rights protests
about certain people
having to sit in the back of the bus,
riding the bus became
a human rights issue,
but not where I lived.

But in Virginia in the 1960s
while my husband was in the military
to protect all Americans,
segregated school buses
picked up only specified students
leaving others at the curb.

Later in my mother's life
she needed home care.
Wonderful, caring Jamaican
women took the bus
to tend to her. When I met them
on visits East, I was so grateful
for the friendship they shared.

Now living West in a university town,
the buses are free to all...just as they should be.
Uber, dial a bus and automatic computer drivers
could make ordinary buses obsolete.
Riding a bus could be replaced
like riding a train for mass transit.
Riding the bus could be for anyone.

Friendiversaries

> The yearly recurrence of the date that two or more people became friends.   Dictionary.com

If you have a lot of friends
this could become unwieldly
with multiple celebrations every day.

How can you determine the date
when you knew you were friends?
How do you keep track?

Did you recognize it with a vow,
poem, commemorative token?
Do you forget broken or friendships lost?

How do you celebrate a friendiversary?
A phone call, party, hang out time?
Gifts? Dining out? Greeting card?

Diversary is in the word so maybe
different strokes for different folks.
Maybe the friendship is not beneficial?

Perhaps friends have agendas
that grow apart–are heartbreaking.
How long do friends stick it out?

Are there any ground rules
for friendship making? How close?
How intense? How mutual?

Perhaps each day a friendship
is gratifying, it is worth the effort
to smile and be grateful.

At the Candy Store Window
Near Valentine's Day

B: Look Nancy, it was just all red and green
and now it is red and white. Even white chocolate.

N: You're right, Barbara lots of chubby cupids
and paper hearts.

B: All kinds of cats, dogs, hearts and cupid shapes.
Wonder if they come in milk and dark chocolate?

N: My stash of chocolate is peppermint patties
and Dove bites. Not this pricy stuff.

B: I prefer plain M and M's. A while ago Dick got some
custom-made with mushy messages. But, he's getting
forgetful.

N: I'm boycotting Hershey since they outsourced
jobs from Hershey, Pennsylvania to overseas.

B: Yes, you have to check where things are made
these days. No saying what can get into them.

N: I hope Hank gets me some chocolate-dipped fruit-
no peanut butter, caramel or marshmallow.

B: I hope Dick avoids coconut, but after over 50 years
together, I have to hope he remembers Valentine's day.
Maybe have to wait for a chocolate Easter bunny.

N: I'll hint to Hank for a heart-shaped box, he knows
what I want inside. Maybe some petit fours for a surprise.

B: Maybe he'll surprise you with flowers instead?

N: I hope Dick remembers, but just in case maybe we
should go inside and pick our own favorites.

B: Probably my best bet. Can't even count on a card.

Mic Drop

mic drop- The act of intentionally dropping one's microphone at the end
of a speech or performance, displaying a bold confidence, that it has been
very impressive or cannot be topped. Dictionary.com

In a TV commercial a man deliberately drops
multiple mics for a not so impressive product.
Our poetry group is giving a poetry reading soon.
Should we aim for intentional mic drops?

What if the mic is stuck in a stand
and the ensemble falls and bonks a listener?
What if the mic is hand-held, lifted in triumph,
slips and knocks water glass slurping poem pages?

I've encountered several mic systems
in my poetic performances.
Many boxes struggle with knobs
not getting loud sound to the mic.

I never heard of mic drops until recently.
Probably some pop musicians fling them
to the floor with a resonating bong.
Hopefully not in anger, but in elation.

We are a bunch of poetic crones
reading hopefully accessible poetry.
I will not speak for their mic dropping goals,
but my chosen poems do not qualify.

What a delight to write a fitting mic drop poem!
I'd love to stand confidently and punctuate
the end of my gig with a mic drop-- like a hand weight
at the feet of the front row. Better get writing boldly.

Sharing Boxes

People are putting boxes in their yards
to hawk free poems and books by bards.
Poets and poetasters send regards.

Some folks select works of prose--
small libraries for youth and adults to propose
other books to read-- new books readers chose.

Some Good Samaritans stock a blessing box
with free food, clothing, necessities offered without locks.
Donated offerings' access – a little unorthodox.

I have had poetry in a realtor box,
have dreamed of an outside mini-library.
I need to design an enclosed cabinet.

One wing will have slots for poetry.
The other wing opens to bookshelves.
In the middle a boxy, blessings pantry.

It will have a rainbow arcing over closed doors.
It will be painted blue with puffy clouds.
Lots of dark chocolate amid practical items.

What a delight to invite passers-by to partake
in what stimulates thought and sustains. I have a bench
made of sidewalk chucks to rest on to munch and read.

To create such a Sharing Cabinet
will require many boxes to check off and fill.
I hope someday it will become a reality.

Whether nourishing body or mind, if we think
outside and inside of the box, we can find
ways to enlighten, share and be kind.

Distributing Sparks*
　　* Sparks: A Soul-Sliver Experiences Earth by Linda Varsell Smith

Two hundred books in nine boxes,
taped firmly, to cut with a knife. Rip open
cellophane, cardboard, bubble wrapping. Recycle.

Get scissors, mailing tape, envelopes,
a print-out of mailing addresses.
Stack supplies on the table.

Prepare for paper cuts and sharp clasp jabs
bleeding onto labels. Get bandages.
Place cut out labels under tangling mailing tape.

When sealing envelopes, lick gluey areas
which do not stick. Close metal clasp.
Still need to tape down the flap.

Put prepared packages into mail pile.
Haul to post office in two cloth grocery bags,
plunk on counter with husband's help.

I sit on my walker waiting to pay postage
as the clerk prints postage labels for each book
to ship to continental USA.

A long slip with cost and travel data,
with total for this bunch of books –done.
She dumps books into a mail bag.

Overseas is another post office trip, alone.
I need to complete tedious slips to fill out.
I have to go to the downtown office.

Again I wait in line, sitting on the walker
books in the seat. Postage costs twice as much as book.
Luckily I handout most books in person.

Some copies go to libraries, Poet House, conferences,
to bookstore, exercise class, writing and Scrabble groups,
to family and friends. Some people come to house for pick up.

The stacks of boxes slowly decrease,
until there's usually two remaining in a front room
later to be stored in a back room.

As I am distributing Sparks
I am editing the formatting of Into the Clouds,
while I am writing Mirabilia.

While Maureen Frank formats and illustrates my books,
I am working on another book
until the book is ready for printing.

Though I can check on-line when books should arrive,
I tend to focus on what I am writing and editing,
so when it's time for distribution–it's an interruption.

Morning Ritual Tanka

Sliding feet to the floor
from my high perched bed–slowly
land and emerge toward light.
> Pit stop. Later brush teeth.
> Enjoy seasonal decor.

Hallway leads to kitchen.
Open cabinet for pill box,
fridge for yogurt.
> Blueberries plunk and stir.
> Water washes down roundish bits.

Two wrapped newspapers
splat on concrete driveway–
third rolled near mailbox.
> I stroll with walker
> pocketing papers under seat.

Read three newspapers.
Clip articles for poem research,
event information, friends.
> Prefer news on paper
> or on TV screen.

Dressing is sore process.
Stretch achy limbs to clothe
reluctant body. Jumpstart day.
> Accessories in place? Comb hair,
> watch, glasses, safety pin, purse?

Check daily calendar,
prepare for commitments and meetings.
Cocoon with computer?
> Fill gaps with writing, info needs,
> emails, phone calls, a good nap.

Most days head to car
open garage door for morning exercise class
Back out carefully.
> Once forgot to lift wet, wooden garage door.
> Wonderful accident! Lighter, push button replacement.

Changing Shoes

Born barefoot–then donned booties,
toddled on soft, leather shoes.

Mary Janes, one-strapped shiners
guided my steps to school.

At the shoe store you had your feet x-rayed
in a small box to get the right Buster Brown size.

I wore loafers with a penny in it
or sneakers with long, white laces.

Then tight-toes, skinny-spiked high heels–
wobbled to walk, dangerously danced.

Back to sensible flats and practical footwear–
now velcro flaps on SAS and tennis shoes.

Inserts bolster my comfortable, unfashionable,
old-lady, crone-care, assisted-step shoes.

Roundabout About My Roundabout

My indoor walker balancer
assists my work and play-
      decorated,
      celebrated-
it guides me on my way.

Eating, writing, walking mainstay,
supplies concentrated.
      Movement reduced,
      access produced
when anticipated.

Draped in streamers-color sated,
convenience-seducer,
      time-enhancer
      play advancer
relaxing-inducer.

A peace of mind-introducer,
mobile station answer
      with handy tray
      for night and day–
my museful-entrancer.

A Backyard She Shed

Do I want to build a She Shed?
A place to read, relax and write,
where imagination can spread,
listen to music, dance or recite.

I have my own office
with computer and books.
Perhaps it will suffice,
despite dusty, cramped looks.

She Shed's handy–
a get-away.
Quiet's dandy–
a place to play.

Alone,
mind and heart thread?
No phone?
Do I want to build a She Shed?

Exploring Intentions
and Marvels

Dove

Who can be a poet
and yet a worldling
in passions and habits?

William Collins

Staying Home Tonight

I think I'm staying home tonight
rather than dream in another dimension,
when my consciousness takes a soul-flight
to more places than I can mention.
> Tonight when I awake, there's no recall.
> I'll go back to sleep–no trip at all?

Rather than dream in another dimension
with strange juxtapositions in an alien locale,
I'll turn on a light and stir my imagination,
search for my muse-ful pen pal.
> I'll play meditative, healing music to sleep.
> In the morning I've commitments to keep.

When my consciousness takes a soul-flight,
or when I junket to a Pleiadian space craft...
instead I awake and begin to write.
I shrug off sleep. My spirit laughed.
> I might as well get comfortable. I'm awake.
> I'll jot notes for my muse's sake.

To more places than I can mention--
there I have found multidimensional wonder.
I go with unknown, unbidden intention;
come back with new concepts to ponder.
> But tonight I'm home in bed
> with no idea what's ahead.

Tonight when I awake, there's no recall
of leaving my body behind,
just wakefulness, tiredness overall
but still a curious state of mind.
> Why did I have a travel reprieve?
> No conscience to relieve?

I'll go back to sleep–no trip at all,
with poem scribbles upon a small notepad.
My computer awaits my beck and call
to record word-play from a cosmic comrade.
> Sleeplessly, nightlight hours whisk by.
> I hope meditation CD brings some shut-eye.

Evening Ritual

To high captain's bed
with double bedspread,
catapult to sleep
from two-step leap.
Land on one knee,
twist slightly
then sit
to read
and write
before
I
turn
off
light
to
hear
sleep-inducing CD.

Awaiting Sparks

Your guardian angels are continuously filtering negativity away from you. Doreen Virtue

Apparently in another dimension
I am also awaiting the delivery of my book *Sparks*.
As I enter the scene I am riding home in my Fit
with my husband, as a woman approaches
our front door. We drive far into the back
of our extended property and park.
I am annoyed we would have to walk
so far to the house and our guest
would have to wait.

Shift scene and my book shipment arrives
as have several writing friends.
Eagerly I open the boxes. The books
in the first box look like the proof.
But subsequent boxes are not my book.
These books are larger and filled with color photos.
I am very upset and in my anxiety
I cannot find the phone number of my book's
formatter and illustrator, Maureen to tell her.

I am in a frantic tizzy. So upset,
I finally awake with two leg cramps.
I am relieved the books have not arrived here.
Did my anxiety, leg cramps and dream
come from my guardian angels' protection?
Maybe keep the negativity in a speculative plane
and hopefully in this existence when the books
do arrive–there will be jubilance?

Was the woman walking
toward the front door me-observing
what could be, but hopefully won't be?
At least in that realm I can move easily
without leg pain. Guardian angels
must have whispered in Maureen's ear
to send me an update on my next book
Into the Clouds. Her e-mail says we are underway.
Hopefully *Sparks* is as well. Arriving today?

And while your at it, guardian angels–
how about my sore knees and the anxiety
brewing on the national and international scenes?

Dream Requests

Before I fall asleep, I request a dream
or celestial visit that is beneficial to me
with worthy insights to share with others.

I am not fond of nightmares and see
no purpose served by being scared
and waking with a non-therapeutic jolt.

I must have forgotten my plea
for a creative cosmic quest,
for this dream was just unhelpfully weird.

I was in a renovated barn.
White walls, no desks but
it was a classroom.

Surrounded by some papers and trinkets
on a table, no chair, I wondered what class
I was supposed to be teaching in a few minutes.

Scheduled to teach four classes
at two colleges, I could not recall
which class this was to be. No notes.

There were no lights until
I found someone to push hidden buttons.
Still no light on situation, barn door open.

My mother and grandmother sat nearby
chatting away sipping tea. They had no idea
what class I was supposed to teach.

I went to a registrar to get a catalogue.
When I returned to the barn/classroom
it was not the current class listings.

At this point I was really lathered.
I moved objects on the desk,
fidgeted with limp, blank pages.

Then the students arrived to lounge on sofas,
staring at me, waiting for me to speak.
I asked them what class I was to teach.

They did not know either.
One held a sheet of his classes
filled with forestry and PE choices.

So why were we all there- clueless?
Two or three students picked up jackets and left.
I stood there in puzzled, panicked silence.

Relieved, I woke up to my consensual reality,
in which I was retired from teaching
and my mother and grandmother deceased.

I suppose I could psychoanalyze the dream,
but why be bothered? Just be glad I woke up.
Tonight I will be **sure** to request, light-filled quests.

Turning 77

Turning 77 has some symbolism according to computer consultations.
   I thought it was just an ordinary double 7 between 75 and 80.
   But numerology has several outlooks and considerations.

Turning 77 is the vibration of a spiritual warrior on a path of light,
   who walks a narrow path with self and soul, who works
   for light with the light, eats, drinks, thinks light.

Turning 77 resonates with divine awakening, mystic traveler,
   seeker, inner wisdom, detachments, universe as one
   and whole– an expanding consciousness un-raveler.

Turning 77 in the spiritual realm is a master of intuition,
   access to Universal Intelligence, curiosity, freedom,
   researcher bringing divine wisdom to fruition.

Turning 77 releases the full expression of personal freedom
   to pursue any whim and experience whatever one's
   curious about.   I'll become adventuresome.

Turning 77 is a time of introspection, transformation,
   awakening, self-discovery and detachment again.
   I'll gain knowledge of myself, renewed motivation.

Turning 77 is a time for meditation to gain clarity and understanding
   of myself for by doing so I will lead a fuller, freer
   happier life.   I have found meditation demanding.

Turning 77 I need to delve deep within myself to find what I've ignored,
   or suppressed, to learn to understand, forgive, and accept.
   I must not fear because the complete me is perfect when explored.

Turning 77 as an angel number has a spirituality and intuition focus
   with a message from spiritual leaders to recognize my wisdom
   and being on the right path to fulfill my destiny–a cosmic locus.

Turning 77 symbolizes deep connection to natural and spiritual worlds.
  I'll be more attuned to universal energies, more intuitive.
  Just trust instincts, be confident in decisions as 77 unfurls.

Turning 77 suggests some leadership with keen senses and heightened
  empathy to make a wise and sympathetic leader. Successful
  decisions and choices will help me become enlightened.

Turning 77 means going forward with an open mind in the right direction,
  able to achieve highest goals, fulfill life purpose and be rewarded.
  Maintain balance and good things find my detection.

Turning 77 is in the destiny position on my astrological chart.
  Charisma, curiosity, wit, scientific analysis, intuition,
  freedom of personal expression on my part.

Turning 77 in Chinese Numerology based on birth date
  adds I'm well-balanced, organized, intellectual and practical,
  friendly -- harmonious relationships I appreciate.

Turning 77 in the Chinese method adds I'm hard-working, set goals--
  achievable, imaginative, make excellent writers, artists, dancers.
  We are romantic, melodramatic, jolly, charismatic, souls.

Turning 77 brings one home to where miracles are every minute,
  where one can fly and dance in the stars while in any and all forms,
  a place of wonder, magic, miracles- natural being seems infinite.

Turning 77 is beginning to appear exciting, stellar, surreal,
  a transformational dynamic with serendipitous appeal.
  Now starts the calculation of making speculation real.

I Prefer to Dance

When I asked a psychic why my knees are hobbled,
I was told to keep me grounded to write.
Who's decision was this? Message bobbled?
Was I complicit in this plight?
        I would prefer to dance,
        stay mobile to advance.

I was told to keep me grounded to write
I needed to focus, to sit and record.
But maybe I did not get my assignment right,
for all my seeking this is my reward,
        to not be able to be on the go
        or travel widely to be in the know?

Whose decision was this? Message bobbled?
Dancing with words not with my body?
Perhaps the delivery was cobbled?
If so, the multiversal web is shoddy.
        But whatever, I no longer can dance.
        Some entity denies me the chance.

Was I complicit in this plight?
Did I sacrifice dance to write poetry and prose?
Did I have to choose this way to enlight?
Was this part of some plan of the cosmos?
        Much as I love word-play and writing,
        is their some soul debt I'm requiting?

I would prefer to dance,
maybe some life time to this lifetime's lyrics?
What a delightful circumstance,
to have an opportunity to transfix!
        Solo in writing or dance, perhaps
        can combine in choreographic wraps.

Stay mobile to advance--
even if sedentary let ideas leap.
Creativity has continuance,
no matter the discipline I keep.
        I see dances on stage and screen,
        dream about what might have been.

Dabbing

The act of performing a dance move that involves posing with one's nose in the crook of a bent elbow at chest level while extending the other arm to the side at or above shoulder level, often as a celebratory posture or other competitions.
Dictionary.com

I'd like to be dabbling in dabbing.
I'd be dancing and celebrating.
A smooth move I'd be nabbing.
I'd need to be concentrating
       on something positive and joyous,
       something artsy and magnanimous.

I'd be dancing and celebrating
some feat of mine or another,
like an arrow in a bow vibrating.
Perhaps my knees would not bother
       my attempts to be pain-free
       and dance my heart freely?

A smooth move I'd be nabbing
at least with my top half.
But the attention I'll be grabbing?
Bottom won't choreograph.
       While stylistically posing,
       I won't be that imposing.

I'd need to be concentrating
on the topic of my dancing attempt
and on getting limbs coordinating
without encountering contempt.
       Despite my good intentions,
       I'd need some interventions.

On something positive and joyous
romping in my head, I'd focus.
Might even envision something frabjous,
try some hocus-pocus.
       Can I tap my feet sitting down
       without flailing like a clown?

Something artsy and magnanimous
would elicit my best dapping effort.
To dance again would be marvelous
for anything I delightfully support.
       A bit awkward crooking my nose,
       but worth theatrics, I suppose.

Dancing to Billy Jean

At Lois' 70th birthday
at the senior center--
walls festooned with balloons
and photo montages, two buffets--
I parked my walker and sat
at a long table to chat and eat.

The musical portion was delayed
due to a missing part in the system,
but soon pre-requested songs vibed
even bouncing balloons on the dance floor.
All the dances carefully selected
so dancers could dance solo.

I tapped my feet sitting down,
swayed my arms, bobbed my head
to recent decades beats.
Some of my favorite tunes
I danced while doing housework
itched my twitchy legs.

Grasping the walker tightly
to keep balance, I moved to dance.
I could not resist Billie Jean.
I could see Michael Jackson
grooving, gracefully, in rhythm.
I forgot my arthritic knees.

Quite a long time since I danced upright,
standing not sitting-- I went for it.
I freed my feet, arms controlling walker.
Lost in the music, my legs ignored pain.
Several greeted my solo with praise
as I limped back to seated dance.

Memories of dancing urges me to risk
dancing around the house once more.
All my dance lessons and dance exercise classes
prompt me to walker-dance, not just walk.
I'll never be a college modern dancer again, but I can
enjoy watching others dance as no walker-wallflower.

Dances of Universal Peace

Dances for Universal Peace started in 1960s in Berkeley by Samuel Murshid Lewis who hoped if the people of the world learned to dance, eat and pray together there would be world peace. He combined faith traditions and modern dancer Ruth St. Denis to create the texts and dances.

Now more than 700 dances focus
on the common threads of love,
peace and unity– a global locus.

Like spiritual folk dances,
interfaith dancers hold hands, form
a circle around musicians-- entrances.

You learn the words, then the tune
so you can sing, then the movements
to put it all together to dance, attune.

It is a way to pray, connecting parts
of oneself to other people with God
at the same time–centering hearts.

Dances honor a variety of religious traditions,
with sacred phrases, music and moves to reflect
faiths deeper-than-differences renditions.

We see world-wide polarization increase.
Creating a dance circle is a method
to internationally embody peace.

My crone voice sings, arthritic knees sit-dance,
I outreach my hands to harmonic air.
I give it my try to give peace a chance.

Enough

I have some regrets, a sense of some opportunities missed, but I am no longer in relentless pursuit of more. I think I have found it # enough.   Robbie Shell

When do we know we have enough--
when a toxic relationship is detrimental
when we've accumulated enough stuff?
When punctured boundaries become incremental?
    When dreams come true, you fulfill quest--
    when do we feel we've done our best?

When a toxic relationship is detrimental,
when do we reach the point to let go?
We hold on trying to be sentimental,
but know we're not in sync with flow.
    Enough comes when situation is intolerable?
    Do we have enough energy to leave when able?

When we've accumulated enough stuff
we gift, donate, realize we've accumulated excess.
Parting with mementoes can be tough,
but have they become remnant trophies of success?
    Saving things until you are dead--
    or share with others while living instead?

When punctured boundaries become incremental
and cause pain to your anxious soul,
you realize you might become transcendental
and move on to another possible goal.
    People pop in and out of our lives,
    bring bouquets, thorns, sporks and knives.

When dreams come true, you fulfill quest
do you push for more or sit on your laurels?
Have you satisfied all wishes you request?
Are you stuck in anxiety and quarrels?
    A new dream, a new quest on the horizon?
    Free agent or automaton?

When do we feel we've done our best--
to care for others, broken free of restraints.
We've achieved and collected, passed the test,
realized we'll never be demons or saints.
    Will it be enough when it's time to leave
    we left strands of light in the web-weave?

Disconnected

Hello, how are you?
Long time since last
call.

We have not even e-mailed.
I don't have a clue
what to say.
Good today?
While away
lost your way?
Are you down and blue?

Impasse

You never email or phone.
No holiday presents or birthday cards.
You just want to be left alone.
You never send us your regards.
    Weeks become months. Months become years.
    We'll remain disconnected, it appears.

No holiday presents, no birthday cards.
No accepting responsibility or own
your actions. We're discards
of your instability to which you're prone.
    We can't apologize for what we believe,
    for the silent treatment we'll receive.

You just want to be left alone.
Do not want any explanation
that does not do what you want done.
No desire for integration.
    Unless we accept your terms–
    while silencing, you're building berms.

You never send us your regards
or appreciation for any gifts.
Any contact you disregard.
No healing as time drifts.
    We've little information of what you're doing.
    Just vague ideas of what you're pursuing.

Weeks become months, months become years.
We fulfill our promises to you.
Yet, we always seem to be in arrears.
We can just hope you'll follow through.
    We hope you find the help you need
    for this impasse is painful indeed.

We'll remain disconnect it appears.
Any chance of reconciliation?
Our integrity interferes.
We won't lie to pander for affiliation.
    Memories of shared, happier times
    are preserved in other hopeful rhymes.

Broadening

The New Year's begun
with joy and fun?
Pure halcyon?
        I wish.

With fairy's swish,
add gibberish,
some cleverish–
        some hope?

Widen my scope
with astroscope?
I'm sure I'll cope–
        somehow.

Resolutions

Resolve to light-gather, energize, maintain up attitude
despite setbacks, remember gratitude.
Even an achy and clunky crone
knows you can't work alone.
I'll cooperate,
innovate.
Glow it
poet!
Yes!

Cosmic Compathy

Compathy: feelings, as happiness or grief, shared with another or others.
Dictionary.com

At the moment I am not sure who
I am to feel compathy with and what
I should know about what's true.
Just what can I do about that?
  Do I control my destiny's plan?
  Muddling through the best I can?

I am to feel compathy with and what
some unknown entity set in place
for me to do and where I am at?
Now Earth and the human race?
  No reason I am gleaning
  to not comprehend my life's meaning.

I should know about what's true?
Intuitively or through rigorous study?
Am I part of some cosmic crew?
Am I just some muddied putty?
  How many lives am I a pawn?
  What lottery ticket have I drawn?

Just what can I do about that
my consciousness landed currently here?
Am I some sentient space pack rat
traveling dimensions, sphere to sphere?
  Did my essence have some say
  or just sparked and sent on my way?

Do I control my destiny's plan
for this life time or any others?
Am I part of some cosmic clan?
Where would I be if I had my druthers?
  Some folks more intuitive than I am,
  believe consciousness is not a sham.

Muddling through the best I can,
I feel like a puppet with invisible strings.
I appear guided by some multiversal partisan
not aware of some important earthbound things.
  So, I am left to dangle unaware
  on fractured earth, in polluted air.

Running Out Of Time

It seems like we tend to run out of time or will before we run out of potential.
That makes humanity limitless then, as far as I'm concerned. And I think that's
inspiring. Ashton Eaton

As the world acclaimed best athlete retires
at his peak, winning every accolade,
for other things his heart aspires,
all his medals have been displayed.
  Time out for this athlete
  bowing out before defeat.

At his peak, winning every accolade
he wants to take another path.
His talents have truly made the grade
and he's ready for an aftermath.
  As we each run our course,
  can we race forward without remorse?

For other things his heart aspires.
We also each choose our groove or shift
to some intention to inspire
us to give our life an uplift.
  In this world of space and time,
  are we limitless, even sublime?

All his medals have been displayed,
have his goals been satisfied?
The decision has been made.
He is following another guide.
  When we reckons with time and potential,
  intention and motivation are essential?

Time out for this athlete?
Limitless his new track and field?
Will he someday feel complete?
What will he empower or yield?
  Humanity is running out of time?
  We hit the limit, face our grime?

Bowing out before defeat--
can our turn around be sustainable?
Humanity's made a mess. Can we retreat?
Is the Earth maintainable?
  Will Earthlings run out of time eventually?
  Limitless potential? We have to wait and see.

Creative Magic

Dreamcatcher

Others have seen what is and asked why.
I have seen what could be and asked why not?

Pablo Picasso

Maya's Mantra

You can't use up creativity. The more you use, the more you have. Maya Angelou

A renewable energy source,
playing chords of heart and brain
for potential of what unfolds,
hear music again and again.

Creativity unfolding, entelechy
powerful as love from higher self.
More important than knowledge
play, sound, art, light - life itself.

I hope Maya's mantra is true.
It truly was for her.
I delight at each insight.
I hope her passion will transfer

The Joy of Writing
Writing is the only thing that when I do it, I don't feel I should be doing something else. Gloria Steinem

In writing my imagination roams.
I spoke in rhyme before I could write.
My mother wrote down my dictated poems.
Writing brings me angst and delight.
 I can abandon any domestic task.
 Just some time is all I ask.

I spoke in rhyme before I could write.
The magic of words sustains my soul.
Sounds and images take flight.
I expand the amanuenses role.
 I believe I am guided, channel thought,
 explore the ideas intuition brought.

My mother wrote down my dictated poems
which I illustrated by crayon.
My poems followed me to many homes,
where I sit and word-play, muse upon.
 I write on scraps, receipts, cards,
 record before any snippet discards.

Writing brings me angst and delight.
I relish ideas. I cherish discovered perks,
to uncover darkness to shed light.
I never know where passion lurks.
 I remain open, not fully committed.
 I want new insights to be permitted.

I can abandon any domestic task,
endure interrupted sleep.
In creativity I willingly bask,
for I have word promises to keep.
 A poem emerges any time or place,
 while grounded or scope outer space.

Just some time is all I ask--
patience, heart-mind connection.
There is a multiverse to unmask,
beyond understanding or detection.
 But still I write my unknowing,
 try to spark my soul sliver's glowing.

Mind in Action

Elizabeth Bishop defined poetry as "mind in action". She was fascinated by the "surrealism of everyday life". Poetry should do more than just say what happened.

As I age and experience less movement,
I dwell in a curious head and heart.
I sense what's real needs improvement.
My discoveries are hard to chart.
For me, poetry is like a dance.
I give surrealism a chance.

I dwell in a curious head and heart,
exploring dimensions, lured by light,
trying to turn the mundane to art.
I urge my imagination toward flight.
Caught in the cloud of unknowing,
I accept my ignorance is showing.

I sense what's real needs improvement.
Earthly existence can be harsh and dark.
Ground rules appear a disappointment.
I seek an enlightening spark,
to learn about Earth's destiny,
and give "truths" close scrutiny.

My discoveries are hard to chart,
based on intuition, dreams, disputable facts.
Science and spirituality are a part
but not the sole sources of my artifacts.
Boundaries can confine. To break free
requires patience, diligence, creativity.

For me poetry is a dance
of word play and mysterious thinking.
I like to see lines prance,
following each idea and inkling.
My essence travels the cosmos- anywhere
and I do not have to leave my chair.

I give surrealism a chance
to reconfigure, conjure new images.
I search for a magical resonance,
to make thoughts concrete on pages.
Poetry is a sensual, cosmic display.
Poetry brings light-hope to each day.

Poetry-Phile

In poetry you must love the words, and the ideas, and the images and rhythms
with all your capacity to love anything at all. Wallace Stevens

Join in the dance of the poets
as they choreograph letters down the line.

Poets can find most anything to love
to embrace, exalt and define.

Word-play is the delight in words
as their sounds and shape combos align.

Poets express and expand ideas
discover how form and thought combine,

re-see visions with sparkling images
re-create with artful design.

Dance with the magical poem's rhythms
as metric feet, syllabics, free verse shine.

Cheese

The poets have been mysteriously silent on the subject of cheese. Gilbert K. Chesterton

Perhaps poets are not passionate about cheese.
Maybe some poets are lacto-intolerant?
Perhaps the taste does not please?
Perhaps poets are indifferent?
      Is it the texture? Or the smell?
      Cheese and I do not do well.

Maybe some poets are lacto-intolerant
or into almond milk or soy?
Maybe only cheese burger or cheese cake adherent
or just not a food they enjoy.
      I like cheese puffs, on pizza-- not in chips,
      not cheese steak, mac and cheese or in dips.

Perhaps the taste does not please?
Poets supposedly like it with bread and wine?
However, some can't digest cheese with ease?
Perhaps in a sandwich of cheese slab and swine?
      No matter what they add to enhance taste,
      to me it is gagging, just adds to waist.

Perhaps poets are indifferent
have moved on from inexpensive meals.
Poets might exist on a pasta or rice component
or drawn to vegan and other foodie appeals.
      Poets come in all sizes.
      Who knows what their diet comprises?

Is it the texture? Or the smell?
Perhaps poets are too distracted to notice?
Just not colorful or stinky enough to dwell
on a chunk of cheese or a slice?
      Maybe they have better things to write about,
      are caught up in ideas or feelings, no doubt.

Cheese and I do not do well.
Don't think about it much, until I saw this quote.
Not much to say about it or tell,
but decided cheese is worth a cheesy note.
      Out of sight, out of mind.
      What about chocolate? Dark chocolate kind?

Blooming Mad

Certain writers, including Shakespeare, Homer, Dante and Tolstoy are essential to any real education. He (Bloom) railed against what he calls the "School of Resentment"–scholars who promote reading texts from the point of view of feminism, Marxism and any other ideologies and who advocate the canon to be more multicultural. Harold Bloom

At 86 Harold is beyond his youthful bloom.
He's stuck in the age of Shakespeare and bloomers.
He wants to teach until they carry him out of the room
in a body bag according to rumors.
      He can teach whatever he wants.
      Don't include my thoughts in any of his vaunts.

He's stuck in the age of Shakespeare and bloomers.
Women and other cultures not white European,
don't belong with his gloom and doomers.
His tastes not exactly encyclopean.
      Ivy tower, male privilege prevails--
      no ideological, political details.

He wants to teach until they carry him out of the room,
impose outdated viewpoints on more modern minds.
I'd whisk him from class with a witch's broom,
remove him for more multicultural finds.
      He can preach to his devoted fans,
      but please don't tie others to his plans.

In a body bag according to rumors
is how he wants to exit his last class.
He recites poems to calm bad humors.
Wherever he's going, he'll teach, alas.
      A Western Canon old codger,
      seems a new reality dodger.

He can teach whatever he wants
but say in the end there's only Shakespeare?
Some include Shakespeare in their taunts,
not anything Bloom would like to hear.
      Women's roles mostly dismissive,
      I prefer women less submissive.

Don't include my thoughts in any of his vaunts.
He's written 46 books. The latest Falstaff
"Before I knew thee, Hal, I knew nothing" Falstaff jaunts.
I prefer diversity and a few more laughs.
      I want to hear the voices of all kinds of women
      not the limited repertoire of moldy-oldy men.

Practice

Practice your art...to make your soul grow. Kurt Vonnegut

Practice what you preach? Practice to grow?
Practice light and dark science and art?
Practice and perhaps your soul will know?
Practice and insecurities will depart?
      Practice to hone a skill?
      Practice whether for good or ill?

Practice light and dark science and art?
Practice whether outcome benefits somehow...or not?
Does practice have a guaranteed counterpart?
Does practice open thought? Devise a plot?
      Whether practicing art or science,
      what guidelines exact compliance?

Practice and perhaps your soul will know
if you are providing enlightenment or fear,
if you are creating progress for us to follow
or if you are destroying what others hold dear?
      Soul growth comes with practice?
      What outcome will the soul notice?

Practice and insecurities will depart?
Are we capable of perfection?
Are we lead by mind or heart?
Will we make the best selection?
      Ask why we practice a certain activity?
      Do we seek some celebrity?

Practice to hone a skill–
something that engages our passion?
Have we a mission to fulfill?
What lead us to this persuasion?
      Practice needs some purpose or goal.
      Become a diamond or remain coal?

Practice whether for good or ill?
Creativity and invention can bring insight.
Will Earthlings become more versatile?
Will our practices come out all right?
      Please practice any protocol
      to enhance existence for us all.

Practice, Practice, Practice

In *Search for Signs of Intelligent Life in the Universe*
someone asks: "How do you get to Carnegie Hall?"
Response: "Practice, Practice, Practice."
Lily Tomlin in her solo show practiced her lines
and delivered them with perfect comedic timing.

Whatever your chosen art, most mentors
suggests you need practice to express your talent.
To make your soul grow requires inner digging
so you can seed your garden, bloom.
Not all manifestations are your best gardening.

Where do soul-seeds come from?
A Prime Creator? Muse? Inter-dimensional guide?
Within our DNA codes awaiting decoding?
Do the codes unfold with focus? Practice?
Consciousness and creativity–soul gifts?

What concept of the soul does one choose
to explore? A soul-spark needing igniting?
A soul-sliver searching for the oversoul?
A divine soul-light experiencing to collect
information for the Akashic records?

Art as soul-expression is one choice.
Scientific discovery is another.
The soul is an adventurer in many endeavors.
I chose poetry. Like Robin Williams said:
"Words and ideas can change the world".

Cradled in Radiance

For you are the clan of creators, we who whirl in the stars aware we are
surrounded and cradled in radiance.   Susa Silvermarie

Light-bringers dance with the stars,
create luminosity from their sparkling essence.
They gather starlight to shine.

The clan of creators ignite each moment,
find the dazzle in the new,
with insight, un-swaddle discovery.

We're nurtured in splendor from the stars,
from cosmic spectacles, from fires
soft glow of candle and blaring artificial light.

Stardust dreams illuminate groundings,
imagination and creativity, cuddle in our heart,
rock our cradle of radiance.

Mad Geniuses

No great genius has ever existed without a strain of madness. Aristotle

Still in force from ancient start?
Psychic suffering conducive to art?
Mad scientists-- sets them apart?

Lord Byron thought writers crazy,
affected by melancholy and gaiety.
Maybe boundaries are hazy?

Three Bronte sisters did pretty well
not like addled brother Branwell.
Gals seemed pretty intact, as I can tell.

When reality looks dingy
musicians tend to get bingy
when rocking out and fringy.

Several singers died at twenty-seven.
Drugs towed them to their heaven.
Two Jimmys and a Janis even.

When dwelling in the edge
it's easier to fall off the ledge
letting death stake a wedge.

Genetics tinkering with the brain?
"Cognitive disinhibition" comes again
in genius and disturbed people to reign.

To be out of one's mind
unquiet, deranged, some find
it hard to think and be kind.

Creative or not the brain's on a rampage
flooded with thoughts hard to cage,
capture in sound, symbols or on page.

Many artists are dedicated and fearless
do not become psychotic and earless.
But like Rockwell encourage nearness.

Elon Musk seems very able
to put out- there ideas on the table
while remaining sane and stable.

Maya Angelou overcame trauma,
enlightened soul, in dance and drama
uplifting poetic panorama.

For every genius considered mad,
we can find some who made us glad
they overcame forces that made them sad.

Somehow genius lets jinn out of the box,
finds creative ways to outfox
jailers ready with their locks.

Creative genius can seem intense
yet their contributions are immense.
To break them down makes little sense.

Dreamers

*Every great dream begins with a dreamer. Always remember, you have within
you the strength, the patience, and the passion to reach the stars to change the
world.* Harriet Tubman

You can have the strength, the patience and the passion
for your dream to come true–but should it?
People can have very conflicting dreams,
some of which are unjust, narcissistic, violent.

The DACA dreamers may confront a wall.
Astronauts' dreams are technologically challenged.
Political dreamers can be dictators.
Artists and writers express an unethical, detrimental cause.

Night dreams can become nightmares.
Day dreams can remain ephemeral.
Perhaps some dreams are not worth the effort
or the dreamer is inept, psychopathic.

Harriet Tubman espouses great dreams
from mind-blowing, world-changing dreamers
whose dreams could enhance the Earth
and all its inhabitants. Who is dreaming now?

How many dreamers are considered universal?
How many are cosmic and star-reaching?
How many dream humanity can become stellar?
How many dreamers do we need for all beings?

Are dreamers including all creatures and creations
as their consciousness concocts their dreams?
What is the effect of their dream's fulfillment?
How many dreamers star-gaze so far?

Can we imagine a dreamland surrounded by dreamy sea?
Can we conceive of a fantasy we could make real?
Is all illusion, dream-shattering, a hallucination?
Is to dream a goal, an ideal, a possibility?

I'm a utopian dreamer who knows disillusion.
Poetry and dance induce a dreamlike state.
But I know when inside those bubbles–they pop.
Dreams are chimera, but I still dream they aren't.

Dream Builders

Mary Morrisey interviewed dream builders
from around the world to learn
how dreams can win over time and conditions.

First create with clarity a specific dream
and see yourself there.
We think on frequencies. Find right one?

Second refuse to stay discouraged.
Confidence and tenacity appear
necessary to create a dream.

Third be more interested in growth
than comfort in service of the dream.
Hard work to make dreams a reality.

As I listen to her TedX talk,
all flush in deep pink dress,
she speaks in earnest, intently.

I sit at the computer, heating pad at back,
momentarily free of knee pain,
thinking about the poem I planned to write.

What dreams do I want to concentrate on?
Mental discovery or physical recovery?
How have I manifested the dreams I've had?

I begin the hot pad rotation- back-shoulder,
knee-knee-shoulder-back as I computer muse.
Have I used Mary's three steps to build dreams?

Rotating heat and comfort as I contemplate
and create, I have no idea if I am proceeding correctly.
Whatever dreams come true–perhaps dumb luck?

Crash Tests

Hazardous driving elicits crashes
and requires accountability. Who
or what caused often lethal collisions?

New laws can use textalyzers to detect
illegal texting while driving at time
of impact and distracted driving.

New twist from the breathalyzer
to see if driver is drunk and can
navigate a straight line.

Deliberate tests with crash dummies
determine seat belt safety, but
do not test human's impaired actions.

Soon mechanical tests for driver-less
vehicles when equipment goes wrong?
What if passenger is drunk or distracted?

Some people could have flying cars
with their drones, maybe dodge
space debris someday. Aerial crashers.

But the Cassini spacecraft, controlled
by humans and computers on Earth
hurled through rings of Saturn.

The big dish antenna shielded spacecraft
from icy particles. 21 more ring crossings
before plunging into planet in September.

Driver-less or not, the vehicle needs
to be controlled to avoid crashes-- like
gimmicks, shields, cameras, mirrors etc.

Deadly crashes on the ground, in the air
test our skills and competence. Traveling
takes risks anywhere in the cosmos.

Flars

I wonder what they'll call flying cars.
Perhaps they will call them flars.

Would a group of flars be called a flare?
Not here yet, but we should prepare.

Trucks and trains are too heavy to fly,
besides they'll block blotches of sky.

Flars will act like umbrellas to cars below.
Mini-clouds following traffic flow.

What shapes will flars be--
winged or more like rocketry?

Aesthetics important for a start.
Would be nice to see bottom art.

Murals or skycapes- abstract or photo
could increase enjoyment in an auto.

If looks like clouds, cosmos, stars
people might delight in looking at flars.

Flars will share air with drone and plane,
clutter sky and walkers could complain.

Will flars fly no-road routes, over no-fly zones?
Over protected areas, hit wires for our phones?

Will each aerial craft type have own height
for airways to avoid collisions in flight?

Will flars be run by computers, GPS?
Will this increase operation and safeness?

Sky jamming, more contrails, noise--
depends on technology a flar employs.

Will flars need to get right-of-way
if close to earth or get in the way?

Where will flars land-- on landing strips,
parking lots, roofs, driveways after trips?

How do we deal with pollution- sight and sound--
alternative sustainable energy found?

Sky is scarred, crisscrossed with contrails.
Drones speckle sky. What happens when flar fails?

Flars not as big as planes when they fall,
but in your yard or on you– who do you call?

Airplanes travel airways quite high,
so less distracting to the eye.

But flars, at ground breathers' insistence
will have to keep their distance.

Distracted drivers even in driver-less cars
have more to look at with patterns of flars.

We have rings of vehicles around the Earth.
Cars, drones, flars, planes, satellites to berth.

What about birds? Balloons? Other non-mechanical sorts?
How will they receive flar intrusion in their transports?

If we all are one and interconnected,
how will these flights be intersected?

With every invention and discovery,
some group faces loss and recovery.

The sky is filled with flying objects.
Any proposal humanity rejects?

Night will blot flars to twinkling lights.
New stars made from flar-lights.

Energizing My Museum

Every object doesn't just hold memories, it is a container of Universal Energy.
If you add an object to your own possessions, you also take on the energy of that
object. Sara Wiseman

My mini-museum is a treasure trove of energy.
Oozing ancestors', machines', hand-crafters' chi.
I select my inanimate possessions with care.
I inherited my mother's needlework, Swedish folk art.

I surround the room with color and texture
to energize memory, uplift joy. I'm no minimalist.
Stuff is to puff my delight and gift appreciation.
I love sharing my space with inanimate vibes.

Thousands of angels-- an updraft of light.
Seasonal creatures out of boxed hibernation
exude energy of celebration. Memory triggers.
Portraits and paintings peer and project essence.

If everything is energy and consciousness
I am never alone. I live among a teeming population.
We are all made of stardust with cosmic connections.
Our universal energy bubbles with a multiverse.

Various energetic expressions and sentience
are possible in stabile not just mobile forms.
Everything should be treated with care and respect.
Everything has a story and enhances experiences.

At times I sit and look around me at all the items--
functional and artistic, which make my life better.
I ponder an individual angel and how it arrived.
I wonder about the ancestor in the faded photograph.

Some claim clutter makes us distracted
from our true calling, true dharma. C'est le Vie.
I will decide if who owned it, made it, or where it's from
contains the energy I resonate with.

The clamor to reduce clutter, simplify
for me would be losing a spark of myself.
Some things I can recycle, donate, but some energies
are too precious to release to the cosmos --right now.

The House of Miniatures
Non-breathers-exhale!
Mobilize the immobile!

My reality is downsized, but upgraded. Thousands
of miniatures of seasonal and perennial creatures
        inhabit my colorful, crowded home—
        a miniature museum, art gallery.

If everything has energy and consciousness
throughout the universe—maybe multiverse,
        inanimates could exhale vibrations
        non-breathers' vibes could communicate while still.

Who knows how much joy, radiance
and creativity miniatures exude?
        On what wave-length could they connect
        on their (to us) static reality?

No need to excrete, no waste after creation,
they ask little of us except, perhaps
        some dusting, some admiration
        of their visual enhancements.

Miniatures draw attention by their beauty,
vibrant characters, artistic flare.
        They dwell among us without intruding, require
        little maintenance. Stalwart stewards of delight.

What would happen if their energy
and consciousness enlivened
        giving them mobility, not needing breath?
        Where would they go? What would they do?

Maybe they don't want to create anything
or utilize all the senses humans have.
        They may not want touch or to feel pain.
        Perhaps they'd see and hear differently.

Maybe they just want to journey into the world
as tourists, find another location where
       they can sing, dance, recite their thoughts loudly–
       never breathless, never aching, just enjoying.

More fragile forms would need protection
from the elements and either stay put,
       migrate to another shelter by animated toys,
       hitchhike under cars, take a train, plane or bus.

If they are in collections like my angels' congregation
and have formed well-organized communities
       they might not feel the need to move.
       Perhaps jiggle their molecules in private.

Other seasonal decorations which are boxed
and closeted, wrapped for parts of the year
       might un-mummy, un-tomb to find
       freedom all year long released from bondage.

My home is a refuge to miniatures clustered
in dollhouses, cabinets, counters, tables,
       hanging on walls, ceiling, perched on any surface.
       Will danglers swing? Will flat-toppers tap dance?

I would hope they enjoy living with me and stick around.
I sing with them, don't handle them much. I'd miss them.
       I try to give each mini a viewpoint.
       None have to hang or stand alone.

They have their own network like Internet,
I'm sure, to communicate room to room.
       They see all the comings and goings. Might gossip.
       We are aware of them, but are they aware of us?

I gaze at them fondly. Record each angel as they enter
the collection, but not folk art and fantasy figures. Recycle seasonals.
       Christmas in our Moon Room has been up for three years.
       Holiday creatures overlap in several places as I age.

They might welcome the seasonal changes and remain
in contact when in forced hibernation while still alert
in my box-filled closet. Energy travels with each one?
All is connected whether we know it or not.

If the inanimates have a vibrational liberation movement
out of our hands, figure out how to make holograms
for a lighter existence or reproduce by 3D printer,
I support their manumission.

If they choose to leave, I will thank them for their light.
If they choose to stay, I will protect them, give them a home.
They may become noisy and roam about,
like a new breed of pet, I'd have to watch my step.

If inanimates animate—new traffic jams like mini-drones.
Perhaps they will have levitation and we'll learn to duck.
Sharing our world with our animated mini-creations
might add migratory clutter, but no discharges or expenses.

Miniatures, made by our hands and machines regardless
of judged quality or origin might cause us to pause
and look at our species and our impact on the world.
It would be wonderful to also be an object of love and beauty.

Non-breathers—exhale freely!
Mobilize the immobile—peacefully!

The Art of Living

*I believe we create our own lives. And we create it by our thinking, feeling patterns
in our belief system. I think we're all born with this huge canvas in front of us and the
paintbrushes and the paint, and we choose what to put on this canvas.* Louise Hay

The art of living could come in several media.
Louise sees painting. I would see a sheet of paper.
Perhaps someone could conjure a choreography idea.
Others might prefer drama or sculptural caper.
Some might see science play theoretical part.
Anywhere in life I'd like to see art.

Louise sees painting. I would see a sheet of paper.
Some do propose we come in with a blank slate.
Maybe I came equipped with pen -- now computer I favor.
My passion for poetry does not abate.
As a child of three I talked in rhyme.
I have been at writing a very long time.

Perhaps someone could conjure a choreography idea--
delightfully dance, then teach all their days.
I am a terpsichore devotee– follow this area,
enviously watching their diverse displays.
I was not gifted as a dancer
but they provide a joy enhancer.

Others might prefer drama or sculptural caper.
I love plays and all kinds of art shows.
Most productions I enthusiastically savor.
Where this fascination comes from–who knows?
What force provides these images and tools?
What energy texts each art patterns' rules?

Some might see science play theoretical part.
Sacred geometry, math formulas create elegant universe.
Concepts yield numbers and images not apart
from art in creation of the whole multiverse.
All around, nature is like origami unfolding.
Architecture has an aesthetic its upholding.

Anywhere in life I'd like to see art–
art in relationships, in the connections to ALL.
But how do we get belief? What doles mind and heart?
Start like singularity? With a chart or free-for-all?
Mystical answers remain a mystery,
but I cherish the art surrounding me.

Knead Slime

Adolescent girls need to knead slime.
Slime is so versatile.
When made at home it's in its prime.
For entrepreneurs it is worthwhile.
    Slime can knead, fold, swirl
    entertains a playful girl.

Slime is so versatile--
glutinous, colorful, based on Elmer's glue.
You can add coloring, confetti, glitter while
adding lotion, soaps, shaving cream too.
    Many young slime-makers have their own recipe,
    to make it noisy, soft, stretchy or fluffy.

When made at home it's at its prime,
though product has also moved to stores.
Girls whip up a batch in little time.
Kind of reminds me of squishy s'mores.
    Must ooze through fingers not too sticky,
    like play dough, not Ghostbuster's goo icky.

For entrepreneurs it is worthwhile
to show sounds on videos, bring to special occasions.
Store-bought slime in craft stores piles,
but homemade brings most persuasions.
    Girls look for slime-suction sound
    and poked "bounce back" rebound.

Slime can knead, fold, swirl.
Fad can relax, handle teen anxiety.
Must be good to look at, whirl
with brand- identity strategies.
    Price is low, but seek high quality.
    Anyone can make it= economic equality.

Entertains a playful girl--
green, gross slime like vomit for boys.
Many slime opportunities will unfurl
from the ingenuity a slime-maker employs.
    Slime's sold at school or after classes.
    Kudos to these hands-on lasses.

The Rock Artist

I am sensitive to the idea of living in the heart of things...a kind of journey inside the stone, a kind of crystallization or fossilization. Abraham Poincheval

Dubbed France's most extreme artist
Abraham Poincheval will live within a 12- ton boulder
for a week at the Palais de Tokyo art museum, Paris.

The limestone boulder will lock two halves.
The two parts can disconnect in seconds
from signal from his emergency phone.

The inside is sculpted to his silhouette,
semi-sitting with a small red mattress
with niches for water, waste and dried meat bricks.

He has been on a diet to lower metabolism
to minimize evacuation of fluids and waste.
He pees in a bottle. He measures his pulse.

His biggest worry is lack of sleep-not claustrophobia.
No watch so he gauges time by museum hours
for no sense of day or night.

He can only move feet and hand inches
yet he does not feel oppressed by the rock.
He feels completely connected to the rock.

We are already locked in our bodies.
He will become the rock's "beating heart".
He expects an emotional roller coaster.

"It's like tripping. It's very complex,
you pass from one feeling to another
like you are carried away on a rock."

Visitors can see inside via infrared camera.
People read poetry, talk to him through the crack,
tell him nightmares and dreams.

He thinks they are talking to the stone
as much as him. He is very happy
the stone has gotten inside their heads.

He will keep a diary which he'll publish.
He finds it hard to explain feelings
to be put down in black and white.

This daredevil for art is a performance artist.
He spent a fortnight sewn inside a stuffed bear.
He ate worms and beetles while living inside the bear.

He will attempt to be a human hen sitting on a dozen eggs.
He was buried under a rock for eight days, navigated
the Rhone River inside a giant, plastic corked bottle.

He crossed the Alps in a barrel, spent a week atop
a 65 foot pole outside a Paris train station, lived
as a human mole and a Stone Age man on small rocky island.

The chip does not fall far from the rock.
His father Christian invented pills that make farts
smell like roses, violets or chocolates.

Abraham's own children age 6 and 8
do not think it weird their father goes
to live inside a rock or a bear.

Abraham's biggest dream is to walk on clouds.
He's worked on it for five years without success.
I hope he survives many mystical journeys.

Circles in the Sand

On the Beaches of Bandon, Oregon

At low tide Sand Labyrinth artist Denny Dyke,
his Circles Crew and Guest Groomers
create Dream Field labyrinths,
smooth, sandy paths through the patterns,
with no wrong turns or dead ends,
just a continuous path to guide your journey.

Since 2015 10,000 pairs of feet
have walked the sandy path.
One man played a Native American flute
while strolling the walkable art.
Since 2015 a hundred labyrinths
have been designed for special occasions–
labyrinths in the wet sand,
carving graceful circles
to walk with moistened feet.

To walk the labyrinth they suggest
take a deep breath, release slowly,
feel the cool sea air on your face,
listen to the sound of the waves,
walk at a comfortable pace.
Be one with your surroundings
and feel the sense of joy, love and peace.

High tide rolls in, nibbles lines
rubs the labyrinth back to the sea.
People stand on surrounding rocks
like Face Rock Way
to watch beauty wash away.

New labyrinths will return
when the tide is low,
to renew art, to pattern sand.
Blank palettes await the curling touches
of Denny Dyke and his magical crews,
the Bandon Beach Labyrinthians.

Wondrous
Spirituality

Sacred Geometry

Ultimately, the word "beyond"
captures the true meaning of spirituality.
In its most basic sense,
going beyond means going past where you are.
It means not staying in your current state,
where you constantly go beyond yourself.
There are no more boundaries.
Dimensions and boundaries only exist
at the places where you stop going beyond.
If you never stop, then you go
beyond boundaries, beyond limitations,
beyond sense of a restricted self.
 # Let there be light.

Derek Hough

Stardust Mission

We are stardust on a mission—
to enchant the world alive
and mate with its mystery.
Sandra Pastorius

Our mission might be to enchant
but some darkled beings can't--
they're not a dazzling inhabitant.

Our mission is to make world alive?
Yes, but we need Earth to help us thrive.
Let's move sustainability into overdrive.

Our mission is to mate with mystery,
to bring art, science, dance cosmically,
to find our way lovingly and peacefully.

Our mission as Earthling stardust,
is to gather, sparkle, not to bust,
to build a harmonious world is a must.

Our mission might lack some clarity.
Somehow we've lost some complementarity
and meaningful connections become a rarity.

Our mission on this beautiful place,
created from stardust from outer space,
is to bring light-consciousness and grace.

Becoming Miraculous

Your existence is a miracle
But don't force a smile
Instead
honor your humanity
Speak in sentences. Kim Adonna

My stardust brain and bones
configured into a human being.
This time around, my heart atones
for all I see disagreeing,
      I want to speak sentences,
      seek some repentances.

Configured into a human being
from cosmic patterns plunked here,
blemished miracles I'm seeing,
bloodied and dimmed by fear.
      When I am realistic,
      It's hard to be optimistic.

This time around, my heart atones
for all the attacks on Gaia
for all the theories and unknowns
for the long awaited Messiah.
      Miracles don't always make me smile.
      To comprehend might take a while.

For all I see disagreeing
with unfulfilled miraculous intent.
I am not currently foreseeing
a time I will be content.
      I'm overwhelmed by extremes
      which overcome so many dreams.

I want to speak sentences
against perceived damage
making people weak with strained senses
amidst the spiraling rampage.
      Did we just come here to fight?
      Turn darkness into light?

Seek some repentances
for all beings placed here to exist.
Miracles can become circumstances
consciousness wants to resist.
      If a miracle does not turn out well,
      some might choose not to dwell.

Explosions of Awe

You are the Mystery without question or answer, and we are the inevitable explosion of awe. Janine Canan

Creation of All is the Omni-Sparkler's mystery.
We are stardust detectives,
incarnated explosions of awe--
to us and to our cosmic creator.

Perhaps we are sprinkles of stardust
which a sentient code patterns
and consciousness lets us experience
for some purpose or destiny.

Awe could soul-splinter all over the multiverse--
separate, re-combine for another tour de force.
Energy vibrating, scintillating in matter...or not.
Bubbles blowing up and bursting awe.

My tiny sparklet of awe looks outward and inward,
contemplating the Mystery,
wondering and pondering, knowing
I can't comprehend the complexity of awe.

Mumpsimus
a person who persists in a mistaken expression or practice (as opposed to sumpsimus) Dictionary.com

I am not infallible or presumptuous
to believe I am strictly correct.
I'd have to be considered mumpsimus.
What more could I possibly expect?
      I can tolerate ambiguity
      probably into perpetuity.

To believe I am strictly correct
would make me considered sumpsimus.
I'm not a good possible prospect,
for I like the mystical and scrumptious.
      I want to remain open to discovery,
      find new pathways for recovery.

I'd have to be considered mumpsimus
in practices, habits and beliefs.
I tend to be mentally rambunctious
leapfrogging to study alternative briefs.
      I'm not fully committed to any idea,
      or to expression of only one media.

What more could I possibly expect
with under-developed faculties still in progress.
I am not always circumspect
or certain of consequences or success.
      I do not even seek perfection
      when I do any introspection.

I can tolerate ambiguity
because I don't have the need to be sure.
Sometimes I don't have the opportunity
to be certain, effective or secure.
      Concepts can change, revise thought--
      change for clarity or for naught.

Probably into perpetuity
quirky, off-trend thinking will prevail,
I will continue congruity
until the cosmos lifts its veil.
      Some perceptions prove untrue.
      Some conceptions I see through.

Dharma

Your dharma is another name for your soul path. When you follow your
dharma, you are following your true soul path, the real reason why you are here
on the earth in this lifetime. Sara Wiseman

We expand our consciousness for dharma.
We try to find purpose and understanding.
Others feel entangled by karma.
Our guidebook is not outstanding.
>Soul growth, your destiny chose?
>What is our soul? I've one of those?

We try to find purpose and understanding,
discover meaning and answer why.
Some of the ground rules are very demanding.
Updates and insights in short supply.
>If dharma is our reason for being,
>some of my essence I'm not seeing.

Others feel entangled by karma,
reincarnated to get it right this time.
Others get lost in Big-Pharma.
Do we ever get Earth's paradigm?
>Maybe I drifted off course in transit,
>don't carry Earth's prerequisite?

Our guidebook is not outstanding.
So many choices of texts.
So many teachers reprimanding,
confusing diverse contexts.
>No wonder Earthlings get off course
>and could make this lifetime worse.

Soul growth, your destiny chose?
You are following a chart you no longer recall?
You left behind other-dimensional clothes?
Plunged naked into this folderol?
>The cosmos is an infinite place.
>Did I really choose the human race?

What is our soul? I've one of those?
A spiritual or moral life force?
I could incarnate again, I suppose
if I don't figure it out, of course?
>Perhaps the Omni-Sprinkler whisked my stardust
>with some intention? Somehow, I might have to trust?

Deliverance

Will humanity's predicted deliverer
into the Golden Age of love
peace, justice and sustainability
be a female? Male? Robot? Committee?
Alien intervention? Vibratory tweak?

We have batches of billions of people
waiting for deliverance.
On this crowded planet,
with high tech in many places,
will the message get out on social media?
Television or radio? Internet alert?
Cosmic blast? Skywriting attention grabber?
Inter-dimensional frequency adjustment?

What languages would it come in?
Automatic translations? Simultaneous transmission?
Gradual electromagnetic waves undulating Earth?
What kind of energy and consciousness
rearrangements would be needed
to create this new reality?

If we are all going to have a chance
to tune in despite the level of technology
and access around us, we probably
would need a DNA code modification
to boost up our vibration so we can
communicate with a higher vibe tribe.

At our evolutionary level- progress has been slow.
As our lack of stewardship becomes
increasingly evident, we need a miracle.
In the past people have sought guidance
from Gods, divine teacher types.
Perhaps this time it will not be a spiritual revolution
but philosophical, political or scientific.
Deliverance might not be divine or benign.

Judging by all our setbacks, some force
is slowing things down. Maybe a battle
over control over us and the Earth?
Positive and negative could duel?
Perhaps ignite another extinction?

When I have read about some options–
I liked the rise of the feminine suggestion.
Most male dominated hierarchies
use male pronouns for everyone,
have rigid glass ceilings hard to break.
Women and certain genders and races
lack empowerment and opportunity.

Since I do not have a vote on a delivery service,
and popular vote might not win,
(they might have an electoral college),
I can't influence the selection for Earth.

Some gurus talk of a 5th dimensional shift.
The criteria for participation tends to be vague
and method of deliverance also unclear.
No precise timing is revealed as well as procedures.
In the meantime we should be nonviolently loving.
Perhaps a Golden Age is an illusion--
a promise-hope to keep the players in the game--
pawns of some super power –cosmic gamer?

In the vast multiverse, perhaps some creatures
have found a formula for a halcyon style of living
inherently encoded in their makeup
that prepares them to exist in harmony
(or perhaps chaos is their preference).
But here on Earth, we are not maturing well.
Wisdom is sparse and the ability to change--
often haphazard. Lots of duds.

Is there some cosmic channel
Earthlings can tune into
offering a delivery service
to benefit all the beings on Earth?
Who would make a global selection?
How could we decide? Do we get a choice?
Where is the originator of the message?
Credentials? Proposal? Project package?

I guess I'll wait for a booster shot
in DNA, while I do consciousness raising
to lift my vibration–just in case
a Golden Age calculation
and calculator service
is actually possible...
But I am not counting on it.

Soul-Snatchers

Instead of making a bunch of resolutions this year, consider making
un-resolutions. Resolve that you'll first attend to your soul. The inner work
always shifts to the outer. Sara Wiseman

Spiritual pundits, coaches, and media sources--
they offer cosmic connecting, soul-tending advice,
how to bring miracles, laws of attraction resources
with abundance/authenticity workshops for a price.
　　Videos with sparkling positive vibrations--
　　they spew to you intentions for all situations.

They offer cosmic-connecting, soul-tending advice,
a balm of calm in these troubling times.
Have you tried meditation, music, some new-fangled device?
How about an e-book, or soul-groupies group that primes
　　all the soul-elevating activities you'll live
　　while you wonder just what they and you give.

How to bring miracles, Laws of Attraction resources,
bridge the abundance gap into your dream life,
how to take quantum leaps, let go of toxic divorces,
free yourself loftily of confusion and strife,
　　lobby guides, hangout with angels, E.T.'s.
　　Many options. Choose what you please.

With abundance/authenticity workshops for a price
promising magic potions, directions to dreams,
some folks can't access or afford paradise.
They watch their lives ripped at the seams.
　　Do these soul-snatchers who claim the light,
　　reach darkness to relieve Worldlings' plight?

Videos with sparkling positive vibrations
advocate with oozing, first free, luring chats,
sound concerned about flickering soul conditions
and ways to clear our souls' habitats.
　　So much time to research these approaches.
　　How do we decide the best-for-us coaches?

They spew to you intentions for all situations.
Basically to set positive intentions for unconditional love.
Words and thoughts can provide hopeful interventions,
Not sure I have found what I am imagining, of
　　a soul-body-heart-mind clinic selection,
　　soul-snatching intuitive cosmic connections.

146

Transformations

Joyful, optimistic, on-line transformers
offer free, teaser videos and recordings
to learn tips to tap your soul,
raise your vibration or frequency
to exude health and happiness
for the benefit of the whole planet–
for the price of workshops or courses
to unveil the perfection of your divine essence,
realize your dreams to gift others.

Gurus, life coaches, psychics, mediums,
card readers, numerologists, runes,
astrologers, alien channelers, angel guides,
courses on miracles and laws of attraction,
other religious and alternative intuitives
have the keys to mastering fear,
violence, suffering, karma, depression...
to unfold love, light, sharing, compassion
to live in the moment as you dream.
New Agers sound like they are on the same trip,
getting people and Gaia in sync
with a higher vibration–perhaps
with the bonus of a dimensional shift
which will cure all the planetary ills
and let Gaia recover from
cosmic collisions, volcanic upheavals
and polluted bio-blasts.

If we can find our inner divinity
and release positive energy
with cooperative, caring consciousness,
we just might avoid apocalypse.
If just a certain (percent varies) level
of consciousness raising occurs,
we will reach a tipping point
so things should be better. But
what if the tipping point is for evil?
We hear about the peaceful silent majority,
but the noisy minority seem to get more attention.

I have listened to many recordings,
read e-books and paper books
in the area of spirituality and it seems
a rehash of ancient wisdom
with some collaborative scientific updates.
I have not yet discovered a program
with enough specifics or provable impact data
that would assure transformation
at the levels we need to face the problems
of the planet and its inhabitants.

Maybe the quest is just part of the life game
and we play different games on different boards,
but I am not a willing participant in gaming or
cosmic experiments without knowing the endgame.
The point of our existence is just a game piece
for some cosmic manipulation?
Are we ingredients in a test tube
dumped on the Earth petri dish
to see what happens–watched by
some curious energy Source. Just what
does the Prime Creator want to create?

My journey for meaning continues.
Transformers have found their answers
and willingly share their discoveries
for a fee for providing guidance.
Perhaps I will find a transforming plan
that resonates with my quirky soul.
What plan implanted my soul,
my consciousness, my rebellion?

Conversing With God

God said to me: If you'll just turn everything around in your mind with regard to those areas in your life that you say are "not working", you'll find they are actually working...the tool is gratitude.   Neale Donald Walsch

When I research various sources
I ask why this planet is "not working",
why there is pain, misuse of resources,
I don't want spiritual knee-jerking–
      miracles with love and gratitude,
      compassion or kindness-- often platitude.

I ask why this planet is "not working"
in a peaceful, sustainable way,
why people seem berserking
during this darkled, destructive stay.
      Neale chats with God, he claims.
      We are to be grateful with God's aims?

Why there is pain, misuse of resources,
greedy, malignant, narcissistic leaders,
is the subject of study in diverse courses.
I'd prefer discovering more light-seeders.
      If each of us has a spark of God,
      why don't we hear more we applaud?

I don't want spiritual knee-jerking--
a relax response or into nowness kneeling.
I'd like some serenity, creativity perking,
more positive, free-wheeling, joyful feeling.
      When blocked, Neale claims miracles happen
      when he moves into gratitude then.

Miracles with love and gratitude
do occur, which sustains faith and hope.
But look around, it's not just about attitude,
so many are overwhelmed, can't cope.
      Accept it's part of our obstacle-filled journey
      to detour and act in this challenging tourney?

Compassion or kindness-- often platitude
spills from some hearts and minds,
I need to up-shift, an uplifted aptitude,
so I can understand and spread their finds?
      Will you please God, sit down with me
      and explain what is supposed to be?

Two Squares

From "Spiritual Obstacle to Manifesting Your Best Possible Life."
Neale Donald Walsh

Walsh suggests there are two squares
on the game board of life:
I am a Seeker square.
I am the Source square.
You discover the magic you already had.

The goal of the game is awareness
to bring God into everyday life.
You win freedom from fear and anxiety.
Spiritual awareness is the secret
behind manifesting.

To begin the game you should acknowledge:
1. Admit to and be aware of a deep belief
        of a divine energy, essential essence
        of the universe–pure energy and ever present.
2. Energy is the essence of the universe,
        effects itself and is at our disposal.
3. Use it and share with others.

If you do for others what you would
desire for yourself, you become the source
person for others. You supply the magic
you already had. Source to sorcerer.

When you are the source of what you want
to experience for others and become aware,
resistance dissolves and you find you
had it all along for a high-functioning,
radiant life, from getting by to getting it all.

Bounce seeker to source square
in a four step process.
1. Identify your highest hope.
      Keep a hand-written journal.
2. Honestly identify expectations that swirl
      in your mind for that hope.
      Demand that it better happen.
      Even get mad at God.
3. Release any requirement of highest hope.
4. Experience living from the source.
      Give to others. Source others.

You need support and community.
Experience what you are coming from.
Information to transformation
takes making it practical with mentor's help
and learning tools.

In playgrounds children play
Drop and Hit 2-square with rubber balls
in two, chalked, five-foot squares.
Children learn underhand position
for hitting the ball, keeping inside the lines.
Learning life games?

When I was young we played hopscotch--
eight rectangles in a chalked pattern
and numbered to tell you where to throw
your object to hop or jump after.
Lots of options to win the game.

Many New Age gurus focus on
laws of attraction and positive thinking,
meditations and affirmations.
Life coaches try to help with what Walsh calls
the big six: wealth, health, relationships,
career, spiritual connection and self-confidence.
The game of life has myriad game boards.
Some of the rules, lines and equipment are harsh.

In many ways I am a square- highly
conventional person, but with inward rebellion.
I like thinking outside the box, but act
progressively, non-violently without addictions
except maybe dark chocolate.

I have played the seeker and source game squares.
I like the role of seeker- exploring the cosmos
and Gaia. Stirs curiosity and imagination.
In the role of source I like to encourage
creative expression especially in writing
as a teacher at all age levels.

I expect to bounce back and forth
between seeker and source squares–
square off in my square dances
not knowing often if I win or lose.
Hope someday I learn if I played the game–
squarely. Fair and square.

But maybe it will be like
cooperative Scrabble– not keeping points,
using each square tile on the squares
of the game board- reaching all four corners,
playing every tile --then place tiles on the tablecloth
making delightful word patterns,
cooperating, making our own rules–
sprawling lines--not all squared up.

Channeling Kryon

Love is the champion of the times. It is the bond of the universe, and is the secret of your unified theory. It is present at the cellular level, ready to be released with appropriate action. It is unconditional, and is unique. It provides peace where none existed before. It provides rest where none was possible before. It is wise. It is the sun within the sun, and is of singular source. There is nothing greater than this. Kryon channeled by Lee Carroll

Supposedly Kyron is a loving entity
who has been with Earth since the beginning.
Took a long time to speak up?
Waited for Internet?

Supposedly readers of Kryon do so
to glean something special, something
meaningful for the longing of their souls,
something to change their consciousness.

Supposedly the human and Earth
are related, interactive, considered
one entity. We are all one system.
Should raise vibration of humans and land?

Supposedly we are to claim responsibility.
Each one is part of the whole. The whole
is experiencing growth. Planetary upheaval
can be unwelcome and unpleasant?

Supposedly ancestors celebrated a growth cycle
in the overview of how things worked.
Apparently humans might view planet
unfavorably during upcoming shift?

Supposedly the majority of DNA
chemistry is information. It is possible
to instruct genes to go another way,
steer to another creative place?

Supposedly 3% of DNA is 3D chemistry.
The rest is multidimensional information.
3% created all the genes in the human body.
All the rest is not understood?

Supposedly humans have linear consciousness.
Quantum DNA does not work linearly.
DNA is not a machine. It totally interacts
with itself–completely? Can change the time frame?

Supposedly spiritually, ancients through intuition
carried "secrets of Spirit" to New Age. Nothing new.
Ancients acknowledged Gaia's energy. Gaia
provided the circle of life and cared for humans.

Supposedly masters came to teach humanity
how to take intuitive abilities to make a difference
for the planet. But humans just worshiped them.
New Age is basic intuitive spiritualism.

Supposedly 90% of DNA responds to consciousness
which responds to Gaia's touch. Science cannot
find a code, system or chemical signature?
The Source does not make junk?

Supposedly there may be a consciousness
that creates life. Is universe biased toward life?
Life is created and destroyed on the planet,
through four billion years–over and over?

Supposedly life returned until system "right."
Then system snuffed life out. Returned again.
Perhaps recreated up to five times. An interdimensional
consciousness glues things together.

Supposedly this creative energy of the universe
is biased toward love? The Lightworker strikes the light
knows how to put things in balance. They put
dark energy in the back seat, don't let it drive them?

Supposedly we have divinity inside, we have
self-healing, solve the unsolvable ability. You can
rid yourself of drama. No worry. Become patient.
Spiritual masters claim you can do it?

Supposedly you have deep pockets for miracles.
You can see interdimensionally. New views
and new opportunities. Step out of linearity.
Mastery discovered and implemented individually?

Supposedly be still and know you are God?
When you do, all will be revealed. You begin process.
Accept who you are. Believe it can be done.
Change the contract to allow it?

Supposedly we each can do it if we want.
Still unclear exactly how to do it and if true.
Perhaps some other interdimensional being
will clue in this 3D creature for a lighter way.

Let there be Light

Do not compete, create. Brian Seth Hurst

Another psychic pundit for releasing fear
to trust your intuition, act out of love.
Life has meaning and is magical, appear
to be light glowing in the dark. Miracles of
　　being present, following prompts,
　　bring joy, vision, clarifying romps.

To trust your intuition, act out of love
means opening space for light.
Giving heaviness, darkness a shove,
shine your inner light bright.
　　Do not cave in defeat,
　　create, not compete.

Life has meaning and is magical-- appear
and empower no matter what is around.
Go to the heart, relax, face the frontier.
Ask for help, faith that miracles will abound.
　　Intuitive prompts are there for the taking
　　to use for any creations you're making.

To be light glowing in the dark, miracles of
your opening heart lead to discoveries.
Get out of your way, connect, take off gloves,
be vigilant of old thinking, embrace recoveries.
　　Feel worthy of love to give it to others.
　　Remember dark night of the soul smothers.

Be present, following prompts
lead you to self-love and creation.
Take the high ground, avoid the swamps.
Don't leave all light to next generation.
　　What if batteries in flashlight are dead?
　　Where will the light come from instead?

Bring joy, vision, clarifying romps
to make this dimmed, grimed world better.
Good intentions and goals, but exactly how
can we move on, create, unfetter?
　　We tend to get lost in distractions
　　and miss the miraculous attractions.

Harmonizing With Our Nature
Six Superpowers Course: Mary Morrisey

We have six superpowers? Yes?
I'd better gather them I guess:
      memory, imagination
      will, intuition, perception
and reason to harness and hopefully address.

You can partake of this on-line course.
Videos and guidebook endorse
      proper process to find success,
      gain focus, reduce fear and stress!
But if I signed up would I have buyer's remorse?

Meaningfulness

What gives meaning to life?...four pillars of meaning: belonging, purpose, storytelling and transcendence. Emily Esfahani Smith

Apparently Sufis lean on these four pillars.
They have a theology to express purpose,
to transmit origin stories, transcendence- explores
ways to be happy, bring joy, keep community close.
    Modern industrialized world –higher suicide.
    Depression and alienation collide.

They have a theology to express purpose,
but not all religious experiences found good.
Isolated without purpose can make one morose,
but one needs an adequate livelihood.
    Only when basic necessities are assured,
    can one wonder if other opportunities can be procured.

To transmit origin stories, transcendence –explores
also what others find-- not ways through religion.
We must look inside for additional insights.
Instances of abuse, suffering, grief are legion.
    We must find connection outside ourselves.
    Find larger perspectives with wider, deeper delves.

Ways to be happy, bring joy, keep community close
also gist of psychological and philosophical strategies
which also have miraculous, resilient remedies to propose.
Can we avoid horrific suffering and tragedies?
    Do we need more caring goals, clarity
    how to advance all people's prosperity?

Modern industrialized world–higher suicide,
people escape with screens, drugs and pills.
Many people feel angry and empty inside,
seek relief from personal, societal, global ills.
    We have no guaranteed prescriptions
    for pain, lost souls, lethal addictions.

Depression and alienation collide
when we disconnect, find no meaningful way
to find purpose and a will to live, decide
the only solution is not to stay.
    Those struggling to survive have no time to worry,
    about pillars for anything, they need to scurry.

A Path to Awareness

And who's to say the universe
is but a single thought
contained within the mind of God?
And who's to say it's not?
If love is the lesson,
then how's the teacher taught?   Noel Paul Stookey Facets of the Jewel

A school of Hinduism called Advaita
is known as the direct path.
It's translated as "not two".
Everything is one, it hath
everyday reality and ultimate reality
not separate as it's aftermath.

Advaita teaches you don't have to renounce
world to become enlightened.
We already have divine presence we seek
so we are inwardly lightened.
We don't need to escape to a cave
to be liberated from being frightened.

In the 1970s and 80s Advaita
became known in the West.
The teaching of Indian reversed saint
Ramana Maharshi advocated we request
self-inquiry, an inward process called "I"
to investigate our personal quest.

We discover beneath the layers
of our busy, egocentric mind,
vast stillness, peace, expansive emptiness.
Untouched, untainted experiences we'll find?
Discover through inner investigation,
with transformation leave false self behind?

Pure intelligence and wisdom is our true nature?
We watch rising thoughts and feelings as they come?
Our true nature is always observing, unchanged,
unharmed. Meditation makes stillness welcome.
It's simply meeting and getting to know this presence,
energy of conscious awareness curriculum?

Magic happens watching this process
revealing the truth of who we are?
Beneath the busy mind, quieted
we discover we are stellar?
Watch drama unfold, suffering dissolve
with act of awareness? Spectacular!

We can instantaneously know the truth
of who we are by asking the question-
"Am I aware?" and watch where attention goes.
Use tools of self-inquiry, your perception
to take you to the truth says Advaita.
Up to you to make the selection.

We aren't separate from ultimate reality.
It's here now, this present moment.
It's possible for everyone this direct path.
But I'd like to make a comment.
This opportunity to investigate is always there?
Under layers of illusion-- peaceful intelligence evident?

Oneness is part of many spiritual concepts.
Who is to say if ALL is really all there is?
Who creates the truth test?
Can we pass some cosmic quiz?
I doubt there is a direct path to knowing.
Is it all part of some multiversal show biz?

My Totem Animal

For over five years a circle of women
studied sacred traditions around the world.
We discovered lightning shamans,
indigenous traditions, contemporary beliefs.

On one occasion we tried journeying
to find what animal was our totem.
The condor was my conduit
to otherworldly connections.

My condor consciousness flew away
as I ruminated and meditated
on other intentions, goals and reflections.
The Monday Night Sacred group disbanded.

Recently, the relay channeler, Marilyn Alauria
suggested we reflect on what resonates, communicates
and get in touch with our totem animal.
By the way, come up with 28 ways you love yourself.

I have lost touch with my condor totem,
can't remember how to contact.
What symbolism, insights would a condor have?
What could I learn about myself from a condor?

Condors are New World Vultures
the largest flying land bird in Western Hemisphere.
The California condor was almost extinct, down to 22.
Last free-flying condors in captivity in 1987. Often shot.

The condors are considered nature's cleaning crew.
They eat dead and rotting meat, dive bald head first
into the carcass. Eat carrion of cattle, deer, sheep,
rodents, rabbits. Poor sense of smell, but keen eyesight.

They can soar up to 15,000 feet, 150 miles a day.
In May 2013 there were 435 condors. 237 free-flyers
reintroduced to the wild. They dwell in caves, crevices
and tree cavities. I do not see condor essence in me.

We had a turkey vulture in our backyard recently--
left only un-identifiable bones. Buzzard picked bones clean.
We had to compost the waste. Big bird came to dine,
left leftovers and did not clear the eating place.

Vultures are kind of creepy creatures.
Condors can be majestic, but rare.
Except for being a meat-eater in the West,
my grace, senses and agility can't compete.

Write 28 ways I love myself? Condor connection
not clear. Maybe the Sacred Circle women could reunite,
go on another journey to update totems, resonances,
and renew spirituality, becoming loving, soul-flying crones.

Startling Light

Perhaps they are not stars in the sky, but rather openings where our loved ones shine down to let us know they are happy.   Mindful Soul

Could stars be soul-lights–
startling lights sparkling peace and awe?
All the splendiferous sentient beings
in energy form- twinkling,
blinking and winking their happiness
in their new realm?

When mediums sense beloveds
who have passed before us,
do loved ones beam this soul-light?
We come from stardust
return via stardust,
wherever we are--some form of star?

It is comforting to believe whether
physical or not-physical
some energy connects us all.
Some multiversal memory
or codes record our experiences
and love permeates boundaries?

Time, energy, consciousness
could exist beyond our comprehension.
Light from stars could ignite our hearts
and open our minds to what is possible.
Some multiversal connector plugging us in
to a cosmic fabric of light waves?

Stars are stellar messengers
even if our loved ones send
messages by starlight ...or not.
The glints of light in darkness
bring hope that soul-splinters
can be happy in some existence.

Surreality

When the reality we have a hunch
might be a reality for many of us
        and we know various people
        experience realities differently
and unknown to us, then
        we add imagined realities–
        fantasies, virtual and enhanced
        equipment, media outlets,
        multidimensional contacts ...
                our poor heart-brains
                will they burst?

Experiencing any of these realities
can be taxing to our senses,
        so escaping to a surreal,
        magical realism can be a distraction
and an attraction to create
a more harmonious existence.
        A world where angels paint
        our sunrises and sunsets,
souped up, polluted clouds become
slurpy and burp out gunk
beyond the atmosphere,
        Gaia breathing freer
        might emit less gas and fire.
Our minds and hearts could dwell
in a cleansed, calmed, clear, lighter place?

Supposedly we have free will
to create our own reality, but
        our surroundings can be a challenge
        and others' free wills could impinge
        on the manifesting of ours.
Some say just go with the flow.
        Sometimes not sure what is in flow,
        how fast and deep it is.
Some say just let go and let the cosmos
        guide you to your destiny,
        intuitively; your reality will uplift you.

Meanwhile I am supposed to have
14 simultaneous, multidimensional lives
        with only one on Earth.
        13 beyond my limited consciousness.
Sometimes in dreams I get a glimpse
        ...perhaps?
Sometimes a shaman or psychic
        peeks beyond the veil
        to give clues to my past
        present and future existences.
Sometimes they hint why I am here
        at this time, this place,
        in this body.
Sometimes they suggest I volunteered
        for this assignment
        despite my puzzlement...

Perhaps I lapse from time to time
        from my Earthly focus
        to otherworldly.

Perhaps I yearn for a life
        somewhere in the multiverse
        which I will reach
        after I have finished this reality
        in its many guises.
                In synch with other lives?

Perhaps I will never get answers
        to eternal questions
no matter how much energy
        I put into any level of consciousness.
The multiverse is vast. Some consensus:
        energy and consciousness are infinite?
Lot of space to lug my star stuff across
        seeking a vacation destination.
                Whew!

Beyond

Some say 2017 is the beginning of the next nine-year cycle.
2016 was the Year of Completion to tie loose ends, clean up act.
We don't start from scratch, but move at more advanced level,
to let go of what didn't work, search for truth and fact.
     Time to go beyond boundaries, limitations.
     Time to ignite luminous civilizations.

2016 was the Year of Completion to tie loose ends, clean up act.
Globally disasters, poverty, wars did not end.
I am not sure personally how to react.
It wasn't a great year, I can't pretend.
     Time to reflect and understand.
     Time to step up and take a stand.

We don't go from scratch, but move at more advanced level,
if we are ready to learn and release status quo.
Any progress welcomed as a marvel,
there are so many directions we can go.
     Time to work toward connectivity.
     Time for compassion and community.

Let go of what didn't work, search for truth and fact.
Research beyond fake news, into deepest intentions,
explore new resources, make a new contact,
Worldlings are in need of new inventions.
     Time to delve into all manner of endeavor.
     Time to create a reality you favor.

Time to go beyond boundaries, limitations
heal, reach out, bring in light.
We can enhance so many situations,
if we have our heart-brain functioning right.
     Time to transcend greed, hierarchy.
     Time to sift through institutional malarkey.

Time to ignite luminous civilizations,
join the light-hearted new wave of existence.
We are waking up with new cosmic realizations
ready to face old world, earthbound resistance.
     Time to embrace being multidimensional.
     Time to go boldly beyond -- be sensational.

Allure of Alauria

Marilyn Aluria lightsomely predicts themes
for each month of 2017. It is January
and lots of cold fear surrounds the nation.
Her gentle guidance and suggestions warm.
I will refer to her insights as the year unfolds.

Overall, we should focus on what you want to create.
Set your intention and live in your heart and soul.
Your learning curves expand and grow to higher levels,
align with what is meant to be. Bring in feeling,
something bigger and brighter with faith and peace.

January we act on inspiration, brain-dump fears.
Clear out energy and let it go. Invite love. Anchor heart and soul.
Discern the truth and see what works. Take reins. Have compassion.
Co-create with guides and higher self outside the box.
Hands hold creation. Bring color to life. Create own song.

February is about love. What makes the heart sing?
Listen to your soul. Listen to own self. Clear hearing.
Work with the A team: angels and ascended masters
to bring truth to you and wisdom from dimensional energy.
Create beautiful music.

March is a travel month. Time for your emotional life.
Navigate your emotional life with your truth.
Anger falls away. Live through own eyes.
Take off mask. Travel outside box to new places.
Hard work can lead to miracles, enhance communication.

April focuses on joy, nature and water, trees, ground.
Shift your beliefs to what you care about, have passion for.
Feel passion of the world with senses. Gears line up.
Vibrational alignment to see another way.
Discover what to have faith in and peace.

May is mother month or nurturing roots.
Deep meditation, prayer of what to do together.
Spiritual creator within. Nurture and release.
Open perspective to new opportunities. Fun.
Gifting self, no fear. Embrace life.

June is for rest and reflection. Quiet, rest.
Look how far you have come. Focus on
heart and throat chakra, the third eye.
Replenish soul and body. Love and teaching experiences.
Creating a miracle weaving of your life. Magical month.

July is hummingbirds- dance, music, party,
socialize with family and community. Celebrate.
No victimization. Master your life. Call loved ones.
Start new things. Weave new dream.
Seek animal totem and ask questions.

August is moon energy. Pay attention to moon energy.
Waking up to new things. Create new dreams and attention.
Time for excitement and fun–WOW. Wolf energy. Amazing
what you can open eyes to say or do, Planetary vibes.

September is to look at friendships and release
people you are distracted by. Be clear and honest.
Let go if not much interaction and not in your vibe.
Get your body moving. (Looks like more exercise.)
Listen to your own truth as you move on.

October is the month of mystery and magic.
The veil gets thinner, not just Halloween.
Vibrational understanding. Consider cleaning ritual
with sage and incense. Talk to Gaia. Speak to trees.
Communicate with nature, be aware of thoughts.

November is for gratitude and what you are grateful for.
Attract what you desire. Where do you want to go?
Welcome new gifts. Harvest and pick what to do and release.
Find own truth and dreams. Connect to source. Open to guides.
Gather people together, feed the energy of love.

December is for heart energy. Give birth to self.
New ideas, new dreams, new ways of being.
Angels around you to sing your song. New song,
another color. Month of light. Put halo on head
with action plan to move world to a better place.

I like this light-hearted, optimistic perspective on year.
It suggests a willingness to connect to guides and heart.
It is a positive check-list to enhance personal growth,
raise one's vibration to higher self and higher good.
The allure of Alauria is light and love.

Psychic Migration

When we all move as one....There's no time we're not deeply affecting each other,
following each other, leading each other, being a part of each other's lives, feeling
each other's feelings, living life on multidimensions, past, present and future all
the same ocean of Now. Sara Wiseman

When we all move as one...
like a school of fish or murmuration
we are in psychic migration.

There's no time we're deeply not affecting each other...
Such is the challenge in 3D dual reality,
but add other cosmic souls–beyond surreality.

Following each other...
Not all ideas and people should be followed.
Certain concepts perhaps should not be allowed?

Leading each other...
Leading others can overpower.
Lead so all beings empower?

Being a part of each other's lives...
Sometimes we have to step away
from what toxic others do or say.

Feeling each others feelings...
Compassion, empathy, love and hate:
Have to decide when to participate.

Living life on multidimensions...
Supposedly we have angels and guides,
other dimensional beings by our sides.

Past, present and future all the same ocean of Now...
All souls of the universe swimming , swarming as one.
Energy and consciousness, can overwhelm anyone.

Self-Care

How many of us in our daily lives
have a chance to reflect on self-care?
How many take time to see our soul thrives?
How many take journey to be self-aware?
What gets in our way as we go?
How can we honor our soul not ego?

Have a chance to reflect on self-care?
She wants us to embrace guilt and not resist.
Take back your power, set boundaries where
you trust and support self, assist
opening to universe, divine power.
Take care of yourself to empower.

How many take time to see soul thrives?
Try strategies to practice presence.
Sit quietly, eyes closed, until peace arrives.
She uses cue word, bathes in essential oils essence.
How many take ten minutes to self-indulge
waiting for cosmic consciousness to divulge?

How many take journey to be self-aware?
Soul-nurturing to find our internal truth?
Are you doing what you love here and there?
Do we enter our own confessional booth?
Undergoing self-reflection
will we find our direction?

What gets in our way as we go?
Lack of action and support?
Are we consistent, do we know
what progress we can report?
If this were your last day,
how happy were you on your way?

How can we honor our soul not ego?
Discover what is significant, find the kernel.
Delve into your truth, learn what to let go,
record your insights in a journal?
Maybe you are not into self-care,
trust yourself to go anywhere?

Arithmancy

*Arithmancy: divination by the use of numbers, especially by the numbers in
names. Also, arithmomancy.* Dictionary.com

I am not into numbers. I'm a letter fan.
I have dabbled into some numbers prophecies
I tend to avoid numbers whenever I can.
I perceive images for reality and fantasies.
>   Numbers don't excite my imagination.
>   Can numbers really be good at divination?

I have dabbled into some numbers prophecies.
From my birth date they calculate my life purpose guide.
Astrology and numerology advocate several theories,
divining cosmic meaning for one to decide.
>   How good are numbers to foretell?
>   Math universal language as well?

I tend to avoid numbers whenever I can.
I don't even enjoy counting Scrabble points.
Remembering phone numbers --not my plan.
With math problems, my performance disappoints.
>   I realize I am quite math-phobic.
>   I should not act so catastrophobic.

I perceive images for reality and fantasies
which I translate into words, then word-play.
I love art, plays, screen shows that please
my curiosity which guides me on my way.
>   I have a passion for words --not equations,
>   to find forms to resonate with my creations.

Numbers don't excite my imagination
but geometry was like a puzzle to solve.
Sacred Geometry has a divine inclination.
I don't like number-play to resolve
>   checkbooks --maybe checklists.
>   Number puzzles I want to resist.

Can numbers be good in divination?
Seems formulas do work in science.
Perhaps there is some astrological indication?
Perhaps numbers and letters form an alliance?
>   If I have a choice–I still pick letters.
>   But with numbers also, truth unfetters.

0010110: Zip Code to the Cosmos

Earlier on when I was quizzing the angelic realms nonstop about how and why Donald Trump even came into the picture, the consistent response was..."For your entertainment Beloved...all is well." Intuitive friend.

Somehow I was not entertained or assured.
I am surrounded by thousands of angels
in my collection, but my vision blurred
at this response and sought other angles.

I turned to Galactic Federation of Light
which proposes positive upcoming energy shift.
Connecting to love will make things right.
0010110 is a cosmic code to uplift.

We are connected to many dimensional lives,
parallel dimensions and universes.
Our part of infinite creative collaboration survives
across space and time in multiverses.

0010110 is an energy wave, numerical code,
a window into planes, part of all is one.
Flow love, increase vibration, information download.
An energy shift is in store for everyone.

We exist for a reason, to create, manifest
collective consciousness for love and light.
Souls are wakening, love is truth, best
to expand, increase frequency, enlight.

We have a vibrational signature, give birth
to lives in multiple levels of dimensions.
Our current focus might be on Earth,
but other realities affected by our intentions.

All happens in respect to new and now.
You are here as part of a collective mind.
Gather love energy and inspiration somehow
and wisdom and enlightenment you'll find.

We are one with an eternal fabric
co-creating on many levels while
existing in an Earth's matrix,
expressing and creating your unique style.

You are eternal on the astral plane,
other dimensions throughout time and space.
Connect with your oversoul, it's plain
you manifest and energize all over the place.

You are always expanding, embraced
on other expressional levels, vibrations.
Your contributions are energetically enhanced,
in myriads of other stellar situations.

0010110 is significant variable to events.
0 and 1 numerical signature, format
for Earth energy matrix to cosmos sent
all over creation, platform for creation- how's that!

Earth benefits from this oneness of energy.
All conscious beings here to create,
connect to higher levels of synergy,
hearts and souls here to participate.

All things exist as part of 0010110 energetic matrix,
expand enlightenment, frequencies and love.
I want to learn some uplifting, inspiring tricks,
for all the layers and levels I'm part of.

Matter is energy and illusion,
can exercise soul with love and creativity.
I am close to the conclusion
I'm connected for infinity.

My oversoul is puzzling for comprehending
why all the chaos, pain, negativity persists.
I am struggling for understanding
why all this is necessary, my heart-mind resists.

Angelic beings, stellar beings of light--
I am not here wanting to be entertained.
I want to assist all to become bright.
I want some peaceful, benign order maintained.

When justice and joy are in the spotlight,
I can be entertained in a world of art and dance,
will write and choreograph newly found delight
about what the high-vibe reality will enhance.

444

Last night after a tall glass of peach ice tea
I was up several times- about every three hours.
When I looked at the clock I saw 444.
I am not a number fan but I had read
about angel numbers and resolved
to check the message in the morning.

The internet suggests meanings for 444.
One consistent theme was angels wanted
to get my attention. Angels are with us always
to send guidance, support, and unconditional love.
They like to be asked for help and somehow
I needed validation of their love and frequency.

444 means pay attention. Listen to intuition.
Listen for guidance, for angels are definitely
with me and my connection to the angelic
realm is quite strong. Maybe that is why
I have a collection of over 3000 angels.
Angels are igniters of light, joy, creativity.

Some numerologists suggest 444 means
all is well. Another alternative belief is 444
is a warning. Angels disagree with an individual's
thoughts, feelings and actions. A cosmic no.
I clicked for my free life path number-- 6
which is why this poem is in sextets.

My life path suggests I am sensitive,
empathetic, responsible, balanced,
intelligent, creative and express with my hands
like through writing. So is 444 to encourage me?
Am I to release all doubt and fear? Trust in angels?
Attune to their vibration by staying in a state of love?

Part of becoming aware of incoming signs
might be the three angels I bought on a trip
to the coast with husband and grandson
the day before Easter. 444 was Easter night.
444 appears as I write daily poem for National Poetry Month.
What highly relevant understanding of system do I write about?

I need to do deep thinking about something.
Be aware what is going on. Am I moving
to a new phase of life? Finding mastery
and empowerment? Am I to let it flow naturally
so to become it and understand it? Learn
something important to be understood?

Suggestions include asking myself questions?
Am I giving less attention to something relevant?
Do I understand the system I'm working on?
This wake-up call to be more aware is received.
My cosmic consciousness needs raising,
but I am not sure exactly what direction to envision.

Signs can come from birds (black birds are relatives
to me when I see them), music, earth angels
saying the right thing at the right time, guidelines
coming in thoughts and dreams. I am to reach out
with thoughts, thank you, gratitude and prayer.
I might not get the answer in the form I expect.

It is comforting to think angels have your back,
surround you with angelic protection, divine
messages, encourage you not to fear.
In the darkness, interrupted sleep, angels
are there perhaps scripting your dreams
for when you return to your slumber.

So 444 can be "Heads up." "Think about this."
"Check the signs." "Understand the system
and follow your gut." "Relevant information
is arriving." "Look more deeply into what's
going on." "Be aware of signs." This will all
make sense when the time is right? When?

444 was a wake up call from my spirit guides.
Angels want the best for me and urge me
to pay attention to the signs around me. So today–
a shamanic friend drops by with two poetry journals
and a concrete angel reading a book with a butterfly.
A hint to fearlessly write my book–time is fleeting ?

It's in the Numbers

Theme of 2017- ready, willing and courage. Year of receiving. You are being asked to ask. Open to receiving in return, to giving to sharing.
Robert Pease, Numerologist

The numbers for 2017 say we are at the beginning
of a new cycle- a year of recovery.
(Recovery from Obama to Trump? Geez, Pease!)

2016 we planted seeds for the new cycle.
In scramble mode, experimented, discarded
what does not work. (Look what bloomed? Pod-peas, Pease?)

2017 we ask for global awareness, correcting course,
into connection with Divine Feminine. What are we doing?
(Grandiose hypotheses, Pease)

Ask is this playing for me? Love life and self?
Be in the present moment. Every moment is first time.
(What's your Trump calculations, please Pease?)

Be who you are. Be your own role model. Bring energy in.
Be your own doer. Time to share your gifts and receive in return.
(Is Trump part of your analyses, Pease?)

You already have it to be fully-realized. You are supported.
Learn the tools, be patient with our pain.
(Is this Trump journalese, Pease?)

We're in the right place at the right time. Ask for help.
Love comes from within us to give it away.
(Just who are you trying to appease, Pease?)

The numbers in the popular vote, did not support Trump
or his cronies. Numbers never lie? Your analyses positive?
(Trump continues to displease, Pease)

Activate your destiny. Align with your Numerological Blueprint,
which has gaps. Discover your numbers and unique frequency.
(We're infected with global disease, Pease!)

Heart Protection

Your beautiful open heart is a healing contribution to the world, and yet it needs
to be cared for and protected.   Doreen Virtue

She hangs out with an angelic clique.
She has suggestions to protect an open heart.
Hearts can absorb unwanted energies, so nick
for these inadvertent intruders to depart.
        Release darkness for light.
        Keep your heart beating to invite.

She has suggestions to protect an open heart.
Shield yourself with a protective bubble of godly light
or envision Archangel Michael willing to impart
his shield to you, or a filter allowing loving energy to alight.
        It is the intention that counts
        when darkling influence mounts.

Hearts can absorb unwanted energies, so nick
with praying a few minutes for negativity to clear
from body and mind. Morning and night stick
to practice of positive meditation to hear
        guidance or take a walk, read a good book,
        talk to a friend or counselor to re-look.

For these inadvertent intruders to depart
requires you to fill yourself with awareness
of divine light and true spiritual identity, be part
of shifting to positive choices, toss despair, less
        putting up with negativity
        and replace with positivity.

Release darkness for light,
sounds good, but perhaps not easy.
In our dual reality, 3D plight
trying to do our best is not easy-peasy.
        Virtue has angelic connections to guide
        her decisions to the virtuous side.

Keep your heart beating to invite--
the highest physical, metaphorical, spiritual.
Try to seek your own insight,
to find your unique protection and ritual.
        An open heart can play a role
        into a loving, caring, lightsome soul.

Angelic Contacts

How do you know an angel wants
to contact you? Rants or chants?

Seeing feathers is one clue
angels love and support you.

Coins found like pennies from heaven in your path
console, reassure when blue or unwell- better aftermath.

Crystals are another symbol you are provided
with love, support and gently guided.

Sparkling light and colors, unexplained shimmers of light
are light beings showing their presence for your delight.

Repeated numbers called angel numbers
attract attention, alert what encumbers.

Sudden sweet smells make angel's presence known
Archangels use flower scent for their cologne.

Sudden change in temperature, warm light glowing.
Or cold yet not uncomfortable indicates angels showing.

Touch like a soft brush against neck or arm,
or back tingling sensation is an angel alarm.

Presence of someone unseen felt in a room
though room is empty is where angels bloom.

Muffled voices, whispers from thin air
word barely understood, angel guidance there.

These are ways to sense angel's essence
in need of angelic comfort, reassuring presence.

Now these are tips from an Angel Visionary.
Or consult your guardian angel if necessary.

We are surrounded by multidimensional beings.
A light-bearing future I'm foreseeing.

Reconnecting to the Angelic Council of Light

Apparently the Internet says I can connect
with my very own, personal
Angelic Council of Light
by simply saying
"I connect with my higher self
and my council of angels."
Now just what am I connecting to?

Apparently each angelic human soul
gets briefed by a Council of Angels
before birthing on this planet
or any other planet. They oversee
the formation of each life before
one enters into it.

Apparently they provide guidance
for our life's purpose or mission,
genetic makeup, heredity line,
challenges you face etc.
(How much input do we have
since we have to live it?)

Apparently they provide
enlightenment for your soul
with messages of hope,
love, warmth and guidance.
You can access them
by meditation any time.
(Our stereotypes are benevolent,
ethereal, divine messengers.)

Apparently the Council of Angels
is composed of 12 archangels
and a personal "mother angel"
(almost the 14 angels in the lullaby).
Each of us assigned to be part
of one or more archangel's
"soul group." (I guess I'm a groupie.
Wonder whose in my group?)

Apparently archangels guide, protect,
inspire, help, and enlighten
so life will fill with much light,
love and learning. Light-workers
are part of these angelic human beings.
(Do I qualify? Seems lot of folks
are disconnected from their angelic council.)

Apparently we have different
vibrations and resonations.
Michael is the great protector.
Gabriel is the creativity angel.
Two are your guardian angels.
Some others could be Raphael,
Uriel, Chamuel, and Indriel.
(Lots of "el"s like angel).

Apparently this is a time
of great awakening on Earth.
We are surrounded with much
love-filled light to assist
en-lightening minds, hearts
and bodies for this transitioning
to higher dimensions for those
who choose to do so.
(What happens to those
who do not choose or know to choose?)

Apparently this process of enlightening
your mind, body and spirit allows
travel to lighter vibrational energies
and higher octaves.
As we meditate we harmonize
with these frequencies,
surrounding us and locking
into Earth's crystalline grid.
(I do believe I am multidimensional
and in the dream state travel diversely.)

Apparently Gaia is a fifth dimensional soul
who chose to descend to third dimension,
who is rising from 3D ashes
birthing a new higher consciousness.
This creation of the New Earth
is a creation of All–Gaia, humanity,
angels and archangels,
ascended masters, Galactic Federation
including interplanetary councils.
(Cosmic consciousness and creation on the job.)

Apparently all are watching
the new creation taking place.
All is happening in the Now.
Simply we are shifting awareness
of it and entering via energetic "portals."
(Sounds good. Do I need to sign up?)

Apparently there is nothing you need to do
other than continue to be light,
forgive everyone everything,
(really that takes saintlike forbearance),
and focus upon this new world being created.
(I've read about the fifth dimensional shift
and New Earth theories. Could it be true?)

Apparently these angelic councils
transmit from the 10th and 11th dimension.
Have they come close and personal
to this planet recently? Long-distance viewing?
Things might look brighter and lighter there.
(I'd like to think my angelic crew is closer,
more hands on and mind-blowing.)

Apparently the Angelic Councils
are committees with light-filled intentions.
Perhaps I should try to reconnect
or have I been subconsciously connected
ever since I entered this plane?

In the Presence of Death

In the presence of death, we must continue to sing the song of life. We must be able to accept death and go from its presence better able to bear our burdens and to lighten the load of others. Out of our sorrows grows understanding. Through our sorrows, we join with all of those before who have had to suffer and all those who will yet have to do so. Though we grieve the deaths of our loved ones, we accept them and hold on to our memories as precious gifts. Let us make the best of our loved ones while they are with us, and let us not bury our love with death.
Seneca

On the back of a funeral program
appeared this advice Seneca wrote.
We sang many hymns she preferred.

At my age there are many funerals
of parents, a child, family and friends.
Many songs to chose to sing and dance.

To lighten burdens is a spiritual quest.
Sometimes sorrow brings understanding.
We definitely join present and future sufferers.

We hold memories as precious gifts.
We can appreciate loved ones still with us.
Death does not bury love.

I can agree with his sentiments.
I do not agree we can lift burdens and sorrows
with understanding alone. We need compassion.

I look at death as liberation.
When a beloved one dies and is without pain,
I rejoice and sing a freedom song.

Since so many people have died,
I am not afraid of death or aftermath.
We must be part of a incomprehensible cosmic plan.

I'll sing "Somewhere Over the Rainbow",
try to be a light-bringer with words and acts.
When my light douses here- onward and upward.

Igniting the Spark

We are here. We come to put a spark of remembrance in you.
Pleiadian message

Humans, a fragment of spirit,
    we intuit.

Enlivened part of creation–
    incarnation.

Spirit eternal, wisdom light
    is to enlight.

Will we gain the hoped for insight?
Wherever people had their start
what did we come here to impart?
We intuit incarnation is to enlight?

Connecting Hope for a
Mirabilous Future

Echo

*My job is to comfort the afflicted
and afflict the comfortable.*

"Mother" Mary Harris Jones

The Anti-Inaugural March

January 20, 2017   Corvallis, Oregon

> *This is not just an anti-Trump protest. A big part of it is creating a space where people feel safe. We're not going to normalize hate; we're not going to accept discrimination. We want people to know they are loved and that they're important.*   Justin Nielson

On an overcast, wintry afternoon
I joined the gathering of protesters
in Central Park a little after three.
People of all ages carried signs,
carried canes, rode bikes, brought dogs,
even a live turkey with woman
carrying sign *"Trump is Foul"*.
There was a huge group–easily
over a thousand people- pink hats,
black jackets, mostly hand-made signs.
A bear carrying a rainbow umbrella.

As we waited for the contingent
marching from Oregon State University
we greeted friends and strangers.
A little girl played hide and seek
meandering through the crowd.
Another young girl offered
free cookies to the congenial crowd.

Signs waved. We were given a sheet of chants
which we used on the march and in the park.
Chants were lead by protesters with bull horns
when we walked to the river along the sidewalk
passed stores with surprised customers.

Large banners, American and Earth flags
arrived with the hundreds more from campus.
All ages swelled the park grass.
We could not hear all the speeches
from the edges as the mic
was not loud enough, but
we heard Native American drummers
and singers from the OSU long house.
I was handed a sign which I balanced
on the foot rest of my wheelchair:
Make solidarity great again!

Chants either single or call and response
filled the air, echoed on the yellow page.
Not our future, not our fate!
Rise! Resist! Love! Create!
Build bridges, not walls!
Love can't lose!
Make America think again!

Listen people to our call–
healthcare, housing, food for all!
No to war, no to hate–
we will not cooperate!
Not by force, not by stealth–
hands off our common wealth.

Show me what democracy looks like!
This is what democracy looks like!
Si se puede!
Hurt just one, you hurt us all–
solidarity is our call!
Sanctuary city here we come, doo dah doo dah (sing)
Welcome here to everyone, all the livelong day.
Fight for life, hear our sound-
Standing Rock is all around.
Palestine, Ferguson, Oregon State-
Rise! Resist! Love! Create!
No justice! No Peace!
Free education for a free society.
You are not a loan.
People rising, no compromising!
Ain't no power like the power of the people,
cuz the power of the people don't stop!
Say what? (Repeat).
Ain't no power like the power of the sun,
cuz the power of the sun don't stop.
They say get back–we say fight back!
We don't want your dirty oil–
leave it safe down in the soil!
Evolution, revolution, got a problem?
We're the solution!
When our planet's under attack–
rise up, fight back!
Eco justice, social justice, time is way past due.
We got vision, we got spirit–make the world anew.

On the yellow sheet of chants
I wrote down some of the signs:
My favorite was- *Take your broken heart*
              and turn it into art.
Keep the Earth healthy.
All immigrants!
Support midwives.
We promise to protect the voices
              that have been silenced (petition).
Love is louder!
Stronger together!
Liberty and justice for all!
Big Pharma!
Healthcare is a human right!
Equitable healthcare for all.
Old white guy for medicare for all.
Show up for social justice!

Public lands belong to us all!
No sanctuary for Fascism!
Listen to the people's call--
              health, housing, food for all.
Our people united can never be divided.
Do not deport DACA kids and families.
End corporate personhood!
We want Trump's taxes!
Move, but not the way fear moves you.
March for our mothers!
Support our mother earth!
There is no Planet B!

Veterans for Peace
Resistance is not futile
Rise up!
Rising tide Corvallis!
Compassion!
Unite!
Be kind!
Don't lose hope!

Just as we were going to march
from the park to the Willamette River,
we had a brief shower. I put on a tarp.
Then the rain stopped and we were
amazed-- a **vibrant double rainbow**
arced over the park.

We did not have a march permit
so we branched through several routes--
riverlets to the riverside.
We clumped for each traffic light.
Only two contrary men en route:
one man gave us the finger
and one shouted "anarchy".
Rumors were that we were video taped
from a car parked en route.
Many marchers took photos.
Passing cars honked support.

When we reached the river and waited
for the marchers to flow from several streets,
more chanting. Then a young woman
asked several sponsoring groups
to answer these two questions:
How will you resist?
How will you create?
Most wanted justice non-violently
for the next generation.
Over 30 different local progressive groups
have formed the Corvallis Coalition
to resist oppression or threats
to their values.

Marchers were welcomed
to the Odd Fellows Hall for food,
more festivities. My husband
and I went to the car
under darkening, moistening sky.
We were ready for the Women's March
the next day in Salem.
We did not watch the news today.
Rain drizzled on the windshield.

She Flies With Her Own Wings
Motto of state of Oregon
Women's March: Salem, Oregon Solidarity Rally
The Rising of the Women Means the Rising of Us All

One of 18 Women's Marches in Oregon
joins approximately 2-5 million marchers worldwide
on all seven continents in 32 countries
and 670 national marches
for a new progressive movement,
for human rights, women's rights and justice,
on Saturday, January 21st at 11 pm
at the capital in Salem, near the flagpole
on the NW side of the Capital Building.

In Salem 4-5000 marchers gathered
on a chilly, rainy, morning.
All ages and genders donned
pink pussy hats and pink scarves,
carried thousands of signs, toted umbrellas and chairs,
listened to songs and speakers
advocating unity principles
for ending violence, reproductive rights,
LGBTQIA rights, worker's rights, civil rights,
disability rights, immigrants' rights, healthcare,
environmental rights, women's rights,
peace and a sustainable planet.

Marchers protest Trump's documented lies,
vulgar and controversial demeaning remarks
and behavior, hostility for women
and women's rights. A poor role model:
belligerent, orange-tinted, white male billionaire.
He's considered a blatant misogynist.
People are marching for a wide-range
of grievances and fear of setbacks.

Men and Women are advocating
for Women's rights and others'
All lives Matter and all lives need
health care, a clean environment,
access to a decent living standard.

People poured over 44 blocks in Portland,
7000 in Eugene. Half a million in DC.
Everywhere an outpouring of protest
against the policies of the man
with small hands, small heart, small mind,
to replace hate with love, inclusion not division.
Four of us car-pooled from Corvallis.
I sat in the front row behind chairs
for the tired or disabled near the stage.
I sat in a wheelchair, covered by a blue tarp,
wearing a purple hat, safety pins on coat
and sweat shirt, comfy wrapped in a lap quilt,
peering out of the hood to record the events,
writing on a notebook under the tarp,
with mittens, getting some soggy pages,
propping my sign against my knees which
kept my sneakers dry.

My husband and friends told me
the signs from the crowd peacefully
joining the march, some singing
protest songs and from time to time chants.
Some of the songs: *We Shall Overcome,*
This is My Fight Song, Eye of the Tiger,
I Am Woman Hear Me Roar,
Blowing in the Wind, Sound of Silence.
Women Get up, Stand Up for Your Rights,
How Many Roads, Where Have All the Flowers Gone,
Times They Are A-Changing, I Will Survive,
What Does Not Kill You Makes You Stronger.
Folk songs with Katy Perry, Beyonce and others.

Signs: favorite: *Proud to be 94 and nasty.*
We are all stronger together.
Well-behaved women seldom make history.
We are watching (big eyes on sign).
My body, my choices.
Respect. Find out what it means.
Girls just want to have fun-damental rights.
Hate has no home here.
I have uterus on my mind.

Symbols of female = male together.
We grab back.
No pussy grabbing.
I'm a nasty woman.
Inclusion is stronger together.
Women deserve equal wages and opportunity.
We march for compassion and inclusion.
Build bridges.
Protect the planet.
Take your broken heart and turn it into art.
Don't roll my rights.
Respect science.
It's the policies not the election.
Lead with Love
Bernie sticker on jacket.
Oregon Women's March tee shirt.
Love Makes America Great
Love Wins.
Women's rights are human rights.
Numbers too great to ignore.
Create from grassroots equality and equity.
Unstoppable together.
Free Melania.
I am not a sign guy—but geez!
Half of Us Held Back.
No hate. No fear.
Love, Respect, Justice for all.
Have hope to believe.
Make America Kind Again.
OMFG.
Pussy Power.
Trump Totally Unacceptable.
Resist.
Keep your tiny hands off of me.
You are ruining my future— Trump is a bully.
Stop messing up my future.
Facts matter.
I march for all people.
We deserve our rights.
Truth not Tweets.

When injustice becomes law, rebellion becomes duty.
Don't corral women in a fence.
Love all.
The future is female.
This pussy grabs back.
My body my choice.
Make America think again.
Protect our public lands.
Real men support women's rights.
Next stop impeachment.
We are one.
Just keep believing.
Dump Trump.
Women unite. We will not be divided.
Freedom is in peril. Protect our rights.
I'm with her.

Governor Kate Brown wore a pink pussy hat
with rainbow ribbons on the ears,
said we were Women's March 17 for social media.
The March idea started with one grandmother
from Hawaii and spread by social media globally.
It became over 670 events nationally,
18 in Oregon, millions attend sister events
around the world. The DC march would be
the biggest since Vietnam War protest.
Brown urged us not be silent,
we must act. Democracy not theocracy.
Separate Church and State.
She advocated getting the Indivisible Guide
available free on-line, sign petitions,
run for office.

A middle-school girl with a middle-age woman
read the considerable list of sponsors
which are available on Facebook.

Some call and response chants:
We are what strong women look like.
We are what democracy looks like.
We are what unity looks like.
Democracy, unity and action makes us stronger.

Cara Kaser, Salem City Councilor urged us
to change the narrative. You are not alone.
It takes tenacity, grit and courage to stand up
for what's right. Volunteer for change.
Keep politician's accountable.
Know that you are courageous and strong
and now is the time to get to work.

Chant: *How do we make America great?*
Trust, respect, justice for all.

BJ Anderson a radical feminist, lesbian,
Buddhist nun and poet who adopted two children
of color said she marches as a warrior
for people's rights, ERA not passed.
Around the globe think of those with you in spirit.
Against rape culture in universities, military,
and White House. Self-defense should not
be a prep class for college.
We love who we want, to change to a humane world.

Two South Salem black girls sang and played guitar
to *"Aint Going to Let Nobody Turn Me Around."*

The Keynote Speaker was Shelaswau Bushnell Crier
whose daughter Zael was the fantastic singer.
She is a former Willamette Law School professor,
Yale graduate, advocate for women, minorities and education,
with a focus on uniting together to protect human rights
both locally and nationally. She spoke eloquently
on the themes of unity and action. She evoked
the film "Hidden Figures" and the Black women
facing Ladies and Colored Ladies bathrooms.
Division is a tool to keep all subjugated.
Planters used division to keep low wage earners--
indentured servants and slaves as well as
Native Americans to feel inferior.
Division can't hold us back.
People and planet over profits.
We have the greatest wealth divide ever.

We must get a seat at the table.
It is our responsibility to get there.
Don't be afraid to speak up.
Prepare your questions and insist to be heard.
Say "Hell no. I'm going to stand up tall."
Use the **Indivisible** booklet for specific strategies.
We are all colored just different shades.
Be there. Be diligent. Come out and join in.
Know what's going on. Keep on it. Be aware.
Take local and individual action. You can do this.
Stand by those assaulted.

Kate Brown applauded the march organization
and the move for justice and Oregon equality.
Chanted: *We must stand, act, together.*
We are stronger together.

Then the march route was announced.
Stay safe. Follow police. Make noise.
Don't litter. Be respectful. No one was arrested.
It was a peaceful march. No traffic lights.
Roads cleared for marchers chanting,
waving signs, marching jubilantly.
We connected with writers from Corvallis.
We dipped into a tunnel with marchers above.
Strangers offered to help my husband
push my wheelchair up the slope.
We were a wet, chilled bunch, warmed
by the passion for justice.

It felt good to be marching again,
advocating for justice. We drove
to Independence for lunch
appropriately at The Pink House.
When one woman was dropped off at home-
all of us saw a rainbow peek through the clouds.

We were part of the DC march which chanted
Welcome to your first day.
We will not go away!
We are America
and we are here to stay.

Globally women chanted:
Women won't back down.
Less fear, more love.
Many women brand Trump
as a sexist, bully, bigot
and oppose his stand on issues
such as abortion, climate change,
health care, diversity.

Ruth Marcus said this is a presidency
of the raised fist not the outstretched hand.
Trump did not win the popular vote
and he has the lowest approval rate
in recent history. He has divided the nation.
He lacks grace, decency, presidential stature.
The world will have to march again,
hold hands, use social media for change.
As his tiny, narcissistic hands tweet,
we will have to peacefully,
but actively protest,
get our hands shaking for change.

"Not My President" Day 2017

Just about a month into Trump's presidency
thousands across the nation
took their day off to protest, march
and attend town halls.

In Oregon there were four permitted marches.
All were peaceful except for a small skirmish
in Portland where there were a few arrests.
Events in Eugene, Medford and Salem went smoothly.

Portland had two rallies sponsored by
We the People: Marching in Resistance
standing in solidarity with immigrants, refugees,
workers, people of color and LGBTQ. No arrests.

In London protesters want to rescind Trump's visit,
labeling him a misogynist, bigot and petulant child.
His visit will demean the U.K. and Queen Elizabeth.
Elsewhere in Europe, Pence does damage control.

Locally about a thousand went to a Ron Wyden Town Hall
held on the Oregon State campus to a supportive crowd.
He faults Trump and will challenge Trump's agenda.
He answered questions and had good press coverage.

Wyden concluded "It's an Oregon message that we
respect everyone, and we're never going to allow
elected officials to leave that respect behind."
Across the country citizens held signs opposing Trump.

> Tinkle, tinkle little Czar. Putin put you where you are.
> Uphold the Constitution Now.
> No ban. No wall. Trump's regime has got to fall.
> Impeach the Liar.
> Hey, hey, ho, ho Donald Trump has got to go.
> Dump Trump.
> Love not hate: That's what makes America great.
> ImPEACH Now (From Georgia)
> This is what Democracy looks like.
> Not my President.
> A Legit POTUS Divests and Shows Taxes.
> Deport Bad Hombres from the White House.

I stand with Rebecca Wolfram of Chicago
"Old white ladies are really displeased."
I hope this is the last "Not My President Day"
for me, the divided nation and troubled world.

March for Science 2017

> Rigorous science depends not on ideology, but on a spirit of honest inquiry and robust debate. Earth Day statement after marches started by Donald trump.

Globally thousands of people
marched for support of science--
a nonpartisan protest against cutbacks.

On Earth Day scientists and citizens
marched to protect Gaia and for research
to better lives on the planet.

Promote policy decisions
based on science and do not
silence public agencies.

600 cities around the world
listened to speakers like
Bill Nye the Science guy in DC.

Those unable to march
could watch on media,
share their passion for science.

Soggy signs in rain,
glistening signs in sun
believe in objective, informed decisions.

*There is no planet B. * Earth's not flat.
*Jumping off a building will hurt
even if you don't believe in gravity.

* Darwin 2020. Gradual change
we can believe in. * There are no
alternative facts to climate change.

*Science doesn't lie, Trump does.
* I'm with her. (Picture of the Earth).
* Try it, you'll like it. (Picture of pie-pi)

* I march for the trees.
* Vaccinate! Fluoridate! Educate!
* We believe in science.

Locally in Corvallis: 4-5,000 marchers.
Portland: a 44-block march with booths
and interactive displays for all ages.

Scientific freedom without political interference,
proclaimed by young and older marchers, lead by
drums, music, cheers resonating around the world.

Marching for a Better World

USA citizens have marched
on the mall in DC and around the country
for many causes for many years.

But with the majority who did not vote for Trump
seeing progress erased by incompetent leadership
they can only speak up and stomp their feet.

People want to be heard. Corrective action taken.
Globally citizens want their government
to fund life-sustaining priorities.

The Women's March with millions
around the world demanded justice,
equality, progressive agendas.

Tax day March protested
for Trump to release his tax forms
and to propose transparent, fairer taxation.

March for Science on Earth Day:
nonpartisan support for free inquiry
for a survivable planet, higher quality of life.

Citizens of the world need leaders
to protect the environment, stop waste
and pollution, promote peace, justice.

If we all could do our part to create a better world,
we might avoid creating our planet's extinction.
We could march in a parade of celebration.

Electoral Aftermath

People are angrily shouting at the negative news.
Despite popular vote they did not win their point of views.
We are stuck with politicians most voters did not chose.
Alternative facts, confusing fake news we must peruse.

Sign petitions, boycott businesses and attend town halls.
Executive orders, cabinet appointments stalls
progressive agenda with less healthcare. No bans. No Walls!
Destructive to environment backward action appalls.

This is not the result surely most people expected
when Republicans electorally were elected.
Dividing groups, attacking others–was hate selected?
People of good will–unite, stand up. Huddle connected.

Writing the Wrongs with Rights

...in a time lacking in truth and certainty and filled with anguish and despair, no woman should be shamefaced in attempting to give back to the world, through her work, a portion of its lost heart. Louise Bogan

Writing the Wrongs is the registered Huddle name
with the Women's March for some Corvallis writers.
Huddles are part of an attempt to mobilize millions
to win back the country and world we want.

Huddles will work together to share ideas
on how to create a more equitable, democratic,
safe and free world through inclusive,
action-oriented, productive, non-violent resistance.

Huddles are gathering in homes,
keeping the spirit of the Women's March alive,
building the movement with a concrete action plan.
The motto is Lead with Love: a movement grounded in love.

We hope to support women everywhere,
to resist oppression and incompetent leadership.
Huddles are registering in the first ten days of February
to define the next steps to move forward.

Huddles want to transform Women's Marches'
energy into local and national action.
They might use successful tactics
of the Tea Party to reach different aims.

This reminds me of the Women's Lib movement
where we met for consciousness raising.
This is another re-awakening for everyone
to usher in a new age without limiting hierarchies.

We are just organizing, recruiting members
in this volunteer no-cost movement
where we create the agenda and share
at meetings and Internet ways to empower.

This Thursday Corvallis Writers will meet
in my home to begin the journey together
to uplift everyone's chances for a sustainable,
just future lead by the feminine.

...Nevertheless, she persisted.

Huddling

*We come together to harness our energy for positive, inclusive, non-violent actions
to move our country and the world to a more democratic and humane place.
Writing the Wrongs members are independent, diverse thinkers; each participates
in ways meaningful to that individual.* Writing the Wrongs Huddle Goals.

We organized our Writing the Wrongs huddle
as part of the Women's March: persist/resist.
The darkened government is in a muddle.
Can three branches progress forward? Co-exist?
    Women gather to share their light,
    empower the nation to do what is right.

As part of the Women's March: persist/resist
we are gathering to get information for action.
For justice and positive causes, we insist
to be heard, without provoking violent reaction.
    Trump and his cronies are degrading like dirty jokes.
    We want to be away from their hands or yokes.

The darkened government is in a muddle
chaos, confusion on best course to take.
The conservative, regressive agenda is not subtle,
leaving rage, despair, injustice in its wake.
    Deeply mired, not clearing up the swamp.
    Republicans loyally vote in his camp.

Can three branches progress forward? Co-exist?
Will they actually provide checks and balances?
Trump's delusional mandate does not exist.
We must hold them accountable, optimize chances.
    Restoration of responsibility is a must.
    We do not have a government we can trust.

Women gather to share their light.
We write postcards to mail March 15th for "Ides of Trump".
We talk, explore resources and insight.
We are committed, dedicated to triumph--
    advocate for democracy, decency,
    oppose Trump's executive orders frequency.

Empower the nation to do what is right.
With all this rage shall beauty hold a plea? William Shakespeare
This Huddle will continue its peaceful fight.
To unlawful and improper acts we don't adhere.
    Trump's national embarrassment, international buffoon.
    We can only hope his impeachment comes soon.

HER-ICANE*

Hold on
to be free, to be heard, to be loved
and remembered...Hold on
and keep
Holding.   Parneshia Jones

Local writers formed a Women's March Huddle
to act for humane place amid current muddle.
        We refuse to be blown away.

Huddles punch power like a hurricane,
empower a HER-ICANE.
        We refuse to be blown away.

We will continue to challenge and fuss
though the government is against us.
        We refuse to be blown away.

Focus on love and the non-violent way
on the same playing fields where men play.
        We refuse to be blown away.

We'll need all the buff we can muster
to reveal masculine bluff and bluster.
        We refuse to be blown away.

We'll hold on, persist and resist
for equal opportunities, peace to exist.
        We refuse to be blown away.

No more limited, inappropriate holding
a global movement we're embolding.
        We refuse to be blown away.

* Term heard from Barbarajene Williams

StarDust Soup

Ancient, current, future matter are blended. Time wrinkles and waves, bends light and dances with space. And there is no geography that is not swimming in StarDust soup. Bethroot Gwynn

As we stand on our wobbly home rock
ready to dive into the murky waters,
womyn want to star-spray the crock
men inflict upon the daughters.
　　　Time for the rising tide of the feminine.
　　　Time to crush hierarchy with the genuine.

Ready to dive into the murky waters
spring empowered womyn to stew the soup.
Cooking up plans to avoid the slaughters
and taking time to cleanse the goop.
　　　Womyn join men of good intention
　　　to globally cleanse, provide intervention.

Womyn want to star-spray the crock,
illuminate conditions for change--
what to hock, clock, block, sock, stock?
What beliefs must we exchange?
　　　Some hope for a cosmic vibe
　　　to go viral from a higher-vibe tribe.

Men inflict upon the daughters
limitations, waste their potential,
dim their light on controlling altars.
All star gifts need to twinkle. It's essential.
　　　Open up heart-mind of all
　　　to provide planetary overhaul.

Time for the rising tide of the feminine,
is predicted by the alignment of the stars.
Any otherworldly assistance could design
earthbound trajectories like shooting-stars.
　　　Luminescence in blasts of light
　　　could renew joy, peace, harmonic delight.

Time to crush hierarchy with the genuine--
increase equality, release creative spirit.
Starstuff, its time to still the negative spin,
be free to express the best we intuit.
　　　Stardust soup with starlit ingredients
　　　could nourish, stir up a stellar experience.

The Gender Gap

A study of 142 countries concluded
170 years before women equally included
in a biased world, harsh and deluded.

Indexes evaluate attainment in education,
political empowerment in their nation,
health and economic participation.

There is some good news to celebrate
boys and girls in school at about same rate.
Health outcomes same as men – approximate.

But women not well-represented in government.
Economic gaps widening need improvement.
74 counties things worse, need upward movement.

31.7% gap needs to be closed world-wide
to achieve universal gender parity, inside
these four indexes to coincide.

More women work, do bulk of household chores,
plus caregiving to children and elderly seniors.
Men do 34% of unpaid work women do, study explores.

Women's unpaid work load limits ability
to earn as much money, grow professional utility.
Working average one hour longer increases disability.

At current rate it will take 170 years
for gaps balanced and end arrears,
reduce globally women's fears.

Gaps narrowing quicker in some places,
Nordic countries stride at fastest paces.
Other countries barely any traces.

Rwanda has more women elected than men.
Equalize assets of testosterone and estrogen–
make everyone an equal world citizen.

Fully Realized

While writing my book "Hidden Figures"... I relived what these NASA women and their generation of black Americans experienced. I also was reminded of the hope that we all share–to be seen and to see ourselves as fully realized. Margot Lee Shetterly

So many lives lived unrecognized.
Life missions not fully realized.
So many lives lost, compromised.

Dreams never found fruition.
Communication without transmission.
Discoveries greeted with derision.

Do we know our life's purpose?
Ordinary or grandiose?
Did we hit target? Even close?

Is full realization just an illusion?
Based on our own or others' conclusion?
No wonder there is so much confusion?

Any progress to planetary betterment,
global or individual improvement
shows signs of positive movement?

Hopefully I'll make some contribution
some light project or good solution
and not add to darkness and pollution.

I don't need to be seen or seek perfection.
I want to make a life-enhancing selection,
but my influence might not find detection.

To be fully-realized would be great,
but what is it I'm supposed to create?
Hopefully something to appreciate.

Stand Up for Women

Writers are not here to conform. We are here to challenge. We're not here to be
comfortable—we're here, really, to shake things up. That's our job. Jeannette Winterson

Dorsa Derakhshani, Iranian chess grandmaster
was removed from the national team
for refusing to don the hijab
for a tournament in Gibraltar.

Her brother Borna
was also booted off the team
for facing off an Israeli chess player.
Ways to stand up.

Some women refuse to wear
a head scarf meeting officials
who refuse to shake their hands.
Who is respecting who?

"Burga bans" in Europe
a start, but some women cave
when they do not support
women in Islamic countries.

Several young, bareheaded Iranian women sang
and danced to a Pharrell William's "Happy" in a video--
were arrested for "hurting public chastity". 94 lashes
and year in jail, suspended for 3 years good behavior.

We hear of genital mutilations, Sharia law,
stonings, all kinds of abuse and lack of freedom.
Oppressed and debased women world-wide need
our support as we fight for equality and choice everywhere.

I think of the black women in "Hidden Figures"
Scientists Rosalind Franklin, Henrietta Leavitt,
belatedly discovered writers and artists--
unacknowledged and ideas pre-empted by males
by their circumscribed lives, by lack of access.

Men need to stand by women's side,
join hands so their children can become
the best they can be, enriching the world
with their gifts and their light.

Ides of Trump

Millions of citizens sent postcards
to the White House protesting Donald Trump.
Protections and progress, he discards;
ethics, fairness, health care into the dump.

He's replaced the DC swamp with sewage.
Incompetent appointments, advisors picked.
Environmental regulations kicked.
Only the rich thrive, lower living wage.

Sustain freedom with democracy's shards?
Nation lead by a mentally ill chump?
Congress disenfranchising for each age?
Can we recover, heal with our wounds licked?

In Lie-Lie Land

The USA's history of oppression and discrimination
crushing civil, justice and voters' rights,
lurks in this swamp of Trump's administration.
They fail to employ oversights.
       In La La Land–tra-la-la- song and dance.
       In Lie-Lie Land- Trump facing the music? Fat chance!

Crushing civil, justice and voter's rights
we get a president who lost the popular vote.
He stuffs cabinet with supporters and alt-rights
with all the ominous thinking they connote.
       This La La Land is filled with incompetents.
       This Lie-Lie Land unleashes destructive precedents.

Lurks in this swap of Trump's administration,
an air of greed with bankers and billionaires.
He appoints donors for cabinet consideration.
The citizens are supposed to think he cares.
       He bans immigrants, wants to build a wall,
       abandons treaties, threatens healthcare, ignores protocol.

They fail to employ oversights
to investigate hacking or appointees' qualifications.
Conway, Spicer, and Miller lack insights
and deliver fake news, lies to a frightened nation.
       A divided, puzzled country can't understand
       what could happen under Trump's command.

In La La Land–tra-la-la song and dance
its a fictional movie not a reality Trump show.
Congress needs to step up, give integrity a chance,
confront blatant deception, alternative facts, know
       to be aware of Trump's executive order onslaught,
       disruptions, chaos they have brought.

In Lie-Lie Land Trump facing the music? Fat chance!
All three branches of government do his bidding.
With impeachment will our country advance
toward trust, truth, sustainability, forbidding
       constitutional flaws to be exploited,
       prevent Trump-Bannon-Pence being anointed?

Cloudland

The sky, a region of unreality, imagination etc.; dreamland Dictionary.com

What kind of Cloudland will USA be?
A land of spacious, unpolluted sky?
A trumped up land of unreality?
A place to give imagination a try?
      A dreamland where dreams come true?
      A country where peace and justice come through?

A land of spacious, unpolluted sky?
Follows regulations to keep pollution at bay?
But we see land fracked, poisoned and ask why?
Resists those who treat environment that way?
      Where have all progressives gone?
      Lost to the greedy everyone?

A trumped up land of unreality--
executive orders divisive, creating chaos,
destroying immigrant opportunity,
dictating tweets for nationalism and global loss.
      Alt-right, incompetent cabinet of billionaires
      all caught in self-interest, lobbyist snares.

A place to give imagination a try?
Creative people can be left out.
Trump throws out a racist alibi
why only certain folk let in, others in doubt.
      Marches and protests against his views.
      Faced with stifled press and fake news.

A dreamland where dreams come true?
Our oppressive past needs redemption.
Acting wisely, compassionately is due.
Current events should not be an exemption.
      Many people have worked so hard for progress.
      It is heart-breaking to see us regress.

A country where peace and justice come through
despite choice limited, blatant negative 'isms"?
Obviously open-minded, freedom-lovers have much to do,
against daily attacks, gathering unbelievable criticisms.
      In Cloudland, gray thunderclouds gather.
      We blue-sky hope for the clouds we'd rather.

#flakenews

#flakenews = big snowstorm   Stephen Colbert

During climate-changeable February
many Blue states are flurried deep
in unexpected snowfall,
causing airports to cancel fights
(adding to Immigrant Ban's on and off
confusion and delays),
canceling college classes,
(campuses started snowball fights
and gave traveling professors and students
more time to try to get back),
adding another snow day for kids,
(who made snowfolks and snow angels
allowing teachers to mourn
confirmation of DeVos).
Bungling businesses becoming
unable to conduct deals
when staff works internationally.

Meanwhile Trump flies
to his Winter White House
in Florida to play golf with Abe.
(Melania--divesting from profiting
from her role as First Lady-- and Barron
join him from Trump Tower-
his New York White House)
so he can escape the loss
of his Immigrant Ban court case,
the mishaps of Conway's
endorsement of Ivanka's
clothing line (ethics violation).

Congress and other government agencies
are snowed in in Washington D.C.
Confronting the whirlwind
of Trump's executive orders
and confirming his billionaire cabinet.
Senate used rule #19 to silence
Elizabeth Warren reading a letter
from Coretta Scott King revealing
Jeff Session's true character.
Male senators read parts of the letter
uncensored. Republicans won't confront
unqualified candidates and regressive legislation.
Meanwhile snowflakes fall
amid fake news and alternative facts,
tweeting Trump melting lobbied Congress into submission.
Democracy rolls up into a snowball
and rolls down Capitol hill.

No No Nonets

Election Payback

I can't believe Betsy DeVos
was confirmed as education boss.
Public schools are in trouble.
She bursts teacher's bubble.
Two women had balls,
bucked protocols,
brought silence,
so hence
Pence.

Trump's Executive Orders

The point of Executive Order
is not to create disorder,
no to impose one man's will
and causing chaos, ill.
Citizens worry.
He's in hurry.
I beseech.
Impeach!
SCREECH!

Stopping Elizabeth Warren's
Senate Speech About Session

For her reading Corette Scott King,
Warren could not say anything
About Sessions–Judge Jeff.
(Perhaps she's too far left?)
He's a misogynist.
She's a feminist:
equal rights,
fair fight,
lights.

Saunders vs Kasich

If Bernie had run against Kasich,
election would be less of a switch,
less extremes and better ends.
Democracy depends
on freedom, fair minds.
Unity binds.
We got a chump.
Let's dump
Trump.

Ban Bannon

Trump's advisor, alt-right Steve Bannon
promotes racist, sexist canon.
We watch Trump's ego enlarge.
Is Bannon in charge?
Alternative facts.
Fake news extracts.
No surprise,
his lies
fries.

Eight Men

Eight men own as much wealth
as 3.6 billion people.
The gap between super-rich
and poorest half of global population
is obscene. The inequity gap is increasing.
Recently 62 people on the planet
owned as much as bottom half:
verified by Oxfam and Swiss banks.

In order: Bill Gates- $75 billion Microsoft.
Amancio Ortega- Spanish fashion house founder
Warren Buffet- financier
Carlos Slim Helu- Mexican business magnate
Jeff Bezos- Amazon
Mark Zuckerburg- Facebook creator
Larry Ellison- Oracle
Michael Bloomberg- former New York mayor

President Trump claims to be a billionaire
and his cabinet contains mostly billionaires,
Congress has probably billionaires and millionaires.
Who is representing the world's people?
All but two of the top eight are Americans.
Some do give back–some not so much.
Could they pay their workers more?
Could they donate more to meet more needs?

This gap is not sustainable.
Occupy is just a beginning of unrest.
Social media can mobilize--
like the Women's March gather globally.
When will the planet say it's exploited enough?
When will the people demand justice?
The old order must crumble.
A new order of fairness, equal opportunity must begin.

Obama's Farewell Speech

Such grace, intelligence, poise and style!
He beams light with his words, his smile.
Scandal-free, with decorum
lead nation with reform,
beyond partisan,
now citizen.
Broaden scope!
We'll cope?
Hope?

Trumpty-Dumpty

Trumpty-Dumpty
sits on a wall.
Trumpty-Stumpty
faces a great fall.
All the billionaire cabinet
and Republicans
can't fix the problems
and make amends.

Trumpty-Jumpty
at rich man's beck and call.
Trumpty-Bumpty
tweets for poor's recall.
More voted against him
which he won't acknowledge.
He only won because
of outdated Electoral College.

Trumpty-Frumpty
if you're a fat woman, he grabs small.
Trumpty-Plumpty
if you're disabled human, et. al.
He deports immigrants,
tariffs for American jobs
pollutes with our resources,
with his unpaid taxes robs.

Trumpty-Pumpty
bombasts numbers of Marchers' call.
Trumpty-Drumty
beats down protesters' caterwaul.
Power to the people?
Make America great again- defend
deplorables and alt-right,
leave kind folk, minorities to fend?

Trumpty-Thumpty
ignores global protocol.
Trumpty-Grumpty
frightens us all.
His tweet finger is also
on nuclear trigger so
if he is not stopped
the whole world could go.
Trumpty- Chumpty, he's cracked.

Old Father Blubbard

Old Father Blubbard
fills cabinet cupboard
tosses his cronies a bone.

When he got there
he was not aware
he can't govern all alone.

Trump's cabinet is wealthiest ever.
His appointments indeed not clever,
unqualified for their role.

Treasury secretary, a Wall Street insider.
Education secretary, not public education provider.
HHS secretary wants health care to roll.

His environmental head denies climate change.
Regulations and protections, he'll rearrange.
Congress needs to challenge Trump's picks.

The list goes on with Steve Bannon—
with his alt-right, racist canon.
Trump's pulls divisive, dangerous tricks.

We deal with Russian hacking.
Our policies are lacking.
National Security Council? Feel insecure.

We are not a theocracy.
Restore our democracy.
Our destiny really unsure.

How many marches and protests?
How many deliberate un-rests?
How many boundaries will he breach?

Does populace understand fully
they elected a narcissistic bully?
How long until we impeach?

The Golden Toupee

The Swedes call Donald Trump
"The Golden Toupee."
Fake news about Sweden puzzled.
They responded "No way."

Around the world he seeds turmoil;
homegrown chaos in his wake.
Ratings low. More oppose than support.
How much incompetence can we take?

Social media, SNL, and Fox news--
not best way to stay abreast.
Stop tweeting and breast-beating.
Give Hillary's popular vote a rest.

He signs too-frequent executive orders
with thick-pointed, gold-plated pen.
Gilds gold and name anywhere he can
to strike greedy, devil's bargain.

While he's into travel bans,
perhaps we should embargo
some of his expensive weekend trips
to winter White House Mar-a-lago.

His cabinet filled with bankers, billionaires.
His alt-right advisors, includes son-in-law.
He is isolated from the people he serves.
His scratchy actions outreach from his tiny paw.

He can't spell well and rarely reads,
yet he claims his office runs like a machine
smoothly- each day in paradise--
that is not how most perceive the scene.

He attacks the press, any challenger,
won't reveal taxes, sever business ties.
The swamp is murkier and deeper
filled with his deceptions and lies.

He likes to build walls, not bridges
de-regulate clean air, destroys landscape,
needs to investigate Russian hacking,
understand climate change debate.

Three branches need to interact.
Democracy is eroding.
With a conservative stronghold
Liberal tempers are exploding.

Fortunately some justice prevails,
Republicans are beginning to question
whether Trump can lead the nation.
Congress open to suggestion?

The golden toupee on Trump's head
is not a halo, refers to a fake.
More a tin man un-redeemed–
heartless and on the make.

Trump's Marital Triumvirate

2/3 of Trump's wives were immigrants...proving once again we need immigrants to do jobs most Americans WOULDN"T DO.
Anti-Immigrant Ban Sign in New York

Wife # 1 was Ivanka
an Olympic skier from Czechoslovakia.
She became a designer and book author.
When she learned of his affair...
she dumped Trump.

Wife #2 was Marla
an actress and socialite from Georgia.
She was the American girlfriend causing
Ivanka to divorce him. After six years...
she dumped Trump.

Wife #3 is Melania
a supermodel from Slovenia
with jewelry and caviar cream skincare lines.
Now she's First Lady in absentia.
Marchers carried signs: Free Melania.

Perhaps his beautiful wives were trophies
and gold-digging their chosen profession,
but his disrespect for women knows no boundaries,
whatever his wives received they earned.
Immigrant or not, they can dump Trump.

As President, Trump bans (mostly Muslim) immigrants
from countries not involved with terrorism here.
His working wives were not banned from coming.
A costly wall will not stop southern immigrants either.
Maybe we should dump Trump?

Free Melania

During the Woman's March
there were signs for Free Melania.
Then, I was thinking more of freeing us all
from Donald Trump's regressive behavior.

But in a dream I am sitting with Melania
and a woman I do not recognize in this realm.
I suggest since our husbands were in a meeting
that we do something together.

The dream erases exactly what we did.
What I remember is, we shrunk Melania
to about 2 inches tall and she crawled
under a rug to our astonishment.

When Trump entered the room and sat,
Melania escaped the rug and ballooned life-size.
She carried a satchel as she walked toward Trump
and served him divorce papers.

When I jolted awake I wondered many things.
Why would our husbands even meet?
They say Melania does not want to be near
Trump and prefers separate beds and states.

She just was awarded $129 million
from a British newspaper which called her an escort.
Some say she is uncomfortable being First Lady--
not what she imagined and her accent is a problem for her.

But I assumed she was happy to stay in her Trump Tower,
weekend in Mar-a-lago at taxpayers' expense,
serving as trophy wife #3 and a success story
for immigrants who her husband wants to ban.

Was my dream some alternate dimension
where she has enough will and money to drop out?
Her step-daughter steps in as surrogate First Lady?
But why put me in this mess. I voted for Hillary.

Dump Mugwump Trump

The arc of the moral universe is long, but it bends toward justice.
Martin Luther King Jr.

Here comes Donald–Duck!
He'll waddle away soon with luck.
He appears as "malignant narcissist" bully,
who lacks competence and character of "Sully".

Or perhaps it is Mickey Mouse
scurrying around the White House?
It appears a Disney surreal world,
or some fictional scenario unfurled.

Sully could land a plane on troubled waters.
Trump would rather grope our daughters.
They say reality is a collective hunch--.
I'm not keen on this swamp-ish bunch.

Or perhaps reality is an illusion?
Wish I could buy that conclusion.
Unfortunately this impact feels alarmingly real,
disorienting, devastating, disillusionly off keel.

What's the solution to this muddle?
I will cuddle with our Huddle,
open up to resistance at every chance.
We can't let this insanity advance.

Snowballing Together

The older I get, the greater the power I seem to have to help the world. I am a
snowball –the further I am rolled, the more I gain. Susan B. Anthony

I am just one progressive snowflake rolling with my Huddle
to throw snowballs at the Trump administration.
Our Ides of Trump postcards swamped his puddle.
I gleefully joined the defeat of Trumpcare celebration.
     Resist, persist will make our nation great.
     We are on a roll to re-negotiate.

To throw snowballs at the Trump administration
is our duty when he launches disastrous disappointments.
Suspect for Russian interference, he's under investigation.
He selects incompetents for cabinet and agency appointments.
     Immigration policies, bans, the wall – oppressive.
     Environmental Protection Agency becomes regressive.

Our Ides of Trump postcards swamped his puddle,
protesting his alt-right advisors, nepotism, outright lies.
Our remarks and marches are not subtle.
He turns to billionaires on whom he relies.
     His misspelled Tweets suggest he's mad–
     also fingers nuclear trigger–egad!

I gleefully joined the defeat of Trumpcare celebration,
after endless meetings, petitions, protests.
We must protect everyone in this nation
from this misguided leadership truth detests.
     At the election he was even outvoted.
     To his impeachment, I'm devoted.

Resist, persist will make our nation great.
Even Trump voters are becoming aware
his integrity, embarrassing conduct grate.
You can't expect help from a billionaire.
     We must revise electoral college system.
     It should become a top priority item.

We are on a roll to re-negotiate
ways to provide fairness, justice for all.
We are on a roll to equitably create
a new vision, a glistening snowball overhaul.
     Roll on snowflakes young and old
     until democracy's again a stronghold.

Snowflake

I do not mind being called a snowflake,
especially when I consider source.
Liberal insulting slur like cupcake?
I'm unique, precious, special, of course.

Bullying, negative connotations
are not the intentions I would like heard.
Sensitive, I seek safe situations,
keep as a positive, beautiful word.

Restore natural meaning, not heartbreak,
not divisive, negative political discourse.
Term for sustaining life celebrations,
snowflakes can fly like a soaring snow-bird.

Mandala Illustrations

by Maureen Frank, The Mandala Lady

"Soulscape" - Frontspiece, Back Cover
from: MandalaoftheMonth.com/2017/08/02/
august-2017-soulscape/
"The search for Self is an inward journey. Go in peace."

"Alpha Centauri" - page 1
from "Egyptian Mandala Coloring Book"
"Be still and know the I am"

"Snowflake 2007" - page 27
from "Geometric Mandala Coloring Book"
"Bright, shining, sparkling light. For all to see. For all to be"

"Tut" - page 53
from "Egyptian Mandala Coloring Book"
"From deep within my soul, to beyond all that is, I am"

"Quill" - page 71
from "Guidance Mandala Coloring Book"
*"In the big scheme of things,
all we ever really need is each other. Namaste"*

"Dove" - page 91
from "In Flight Mandala Coloring Book"
"May peace prevail on Earth"

"Dreamcatcher" - page 111
from "In Fight Mandala Coloring Book"
"Let me make my wishes, hopes, and dreams a reality."

"Sacred Geometry" - page 137
from "Geometric Mandala Coloring Book"
*"Holy is Thy Name. Blessed is Thy Soul.
Sacred is Thy Source. All this and more, I am"*

"Echo" - page 185
from "Of the Sky Mandala Coloring Book"
"Speak from the Heart. Listen with the Heart"

"Wings" - page 227
Original Art; design is from:
"In Fight Mandala Coloring Book"
*"I can fly away. I can stay in place.
Either way, I know I'm okay."*

"Traveling Along the Space Hwy" - Cover
Original Art
"Relax and enjoy the ride"

Mandala Coloring Books can be found at
TheMandalaLady.etsy.com

Original Mandala Art can be found at
MandalaLady.com

Acknowledgments

Other Poetry Books by Linda Varsell Smith

Cinqueries: A Cluster of Cinquos and Lanterns
Fibs and Other Truths
Black Stars on a White Sky
Poems That Count
Poems That Count Too
*Winging-It New and Selected Poems
*Red Cape Capers: Playful Backyard Meditations
*Star Stuff: A Soul- Splinter Experiences the Cosmos
*Light-Headed: A Soul-Splinter Experiences Light
*Sparks: A Soul-Splinter Experiences Earth
*Into the Clouds: Seeking Silver Linings

* Lulu.com/spotlight/rainbowcom

Chapbooks

Being Cosmic
Intra-space Chronicles
Light-Headed
Red Cape Capers

On-Line Web-site Books:
Free Access @ www.rainbowcommunications.org

Syllable of Velvet
Word-Playful
Poetluck

Anthologies

The Second Genesis
Branches
Poetic License
Poetic License 2015
Jubillee
The Eloquent Umbrella

Twelve Novels in the Rainbow Chronicle Series.